THE TR~~IAL OF~~
PRESIDENT GEORGE II

THE TRAGEDY OF PRESIDENT GEORGE II[*]

BY

JAMES G. MOOSE

Cover Art by Brian Groppe

The Tragedy of President George II tells
the epic story of the two Bush Presidencies.

Using words that Shakespeare created for his
English Kings Henry IV and Henry V,
the play depicts the wars and rebellions of
American Presidents George I and George II.

The play is both a celebration of, and tribute to,
Shakespeare's history plays, and uses their language,
slightly modernized, in every scene and speech.

As the strikingly similar power struggles
of the Plantagenets and Bushes reveal,
the means by which the mighty maintain
their dominion change little with time.

To Kirstie

Dramatis Personae

Chorus   *(Chorus)*

President George I, President of America   *(George I)*

James of Houston, counselor to George I   *(James)*

Colin of New York, army General under   *(Colin)*
                      George I; later Minister
                      of State under George II

Richard of Wyoming, war minister of George I; *(Richard)*
                       later Vice President
                       under George II

Sir John Pikestaff, companion of Prince George *(Jack)*

Prince George, later *President George II*,   *(Prince* and,
                       President of America   later, *George II)*

Patrick the Pundit, rebel claimant of the   *(Patrick)*
                       American crown

Jeffrey, counselor to Patrick the Pundit   *(Jeffrey)*

Bishop Gerald, Bishop of Lynchburg   *(Gerald)*

Jeb, second son of George I   *(Jeb)*

William of Clinton, rebel leader and   *(Clinton)*
                       later President

Angry Citizen, part of a mob critical   (*Angry Citizen*)
                of President George I

Merchant, defender of President George I   (*Merchant*)

Dick the Butcher, part of a mob supportive   (*Dick*)
                of William of Clinton

Queen Barbara, First Lady of America   (*Barbara*)
                married to George I

Tournament Chairman   (*Chairman*)

Tournament Marshal   (*Marshal*)

John of Arizona, claimant to American crown   (*John*)

Donald of Illinois, war minister under George II (*Donald*)

Condoleezza, Countess of Stanford, Presidential (*Condi*)
                                Adviser

Babylonian Ambassador   (*Ambassador*)

Barack of Chicago, rebel and future President   (*Barack*)

Saddam, Sultan of Babylon   (*Saddam*)

Uday, son of Saddam   (*Uday*)

Tariq, state minister of Babylon   (*Tariq*)

Messenger, retainer of Saddam   (*Messenger*)

Sergeant, soldier serving President George II   (*Sergeant*)

Mayor of Fallujah, loyalist of Saddam   (*Mayor*)

Envoy, messenger with information   (*Envoy*)
        from Babylon

Sarah, Countess of Alaska, schemer and   (*Sarah*)
                              conspirator

Soldier, soldier serving Barack   (*Soldier*)

SCENE.—America and Mesopotamia.

PROLOGUE

[ENTER CHORUS]

Chorus. Welcome, friends, and thank you all for coming.
I am the Chorus to this history,
in which our actors use archaic speech
in reenacting a modern drama.
My first duty, as your guide through our play,
is to humbly beg your grace and pardon;
for my colleagues and I are unworthy
heralds of the story we dare to tell,
in which great nations clash fiercely in war,
their mighty leaders mortal enemies.

How I wish I had the power to make
this small stage worthy of our great purpose!
Oh, for a fiery Muse that could fly to
Heaven and bring me back such a power!
Our scenes would swell beyond this close setting;
our players would loom like fighting titans.

But as I see no such obliging Muse,
I must beseech your imaginations:
Envision the entire globe as our stage!
Picture colossal, heroic figures.
Conjure the sight of young President George
assuming the warlike mantle of Mars.
See famine, sword, and fire crouch at his heels,
like hell-hounds to be unleashed on his foes.
Imagine the Mesopotamian
sun glistening on a sea of helmets,
and visualize thousands of horses
raising swirling clouds of hot, blinding dust.

Next, suspend your disbelief as you hear
our characters use language that is clear,
and even poetic, in conveying
their most profound and awful sentiments.
Accept the conceit that even the most
uneducated, inarticulate
persons can sometimes speak with golden tongues,
their thoughts more dignified than expected.
Believe, too, that even the most hateful,
evil villains can sometimes speak the truth.

Further, indulge the fiction that events
lasting years can be portrayed in just hours.

Having given you this unsought advice,
I leave you now to watch, and judge, our play.
We begin many years ago, when the
old President George still held the scepter.
          [EXIT CHORUS]

SCENE.—America.

Act I. Scene I.—Washington. The Palace.

> *[ENTER PRESIDENT GEORGE I, RICHARD OF
> WYOMING, COLIN OF NEW YORK, AND OTHERS]*

George I. We are so shaken by these civil broils,
and so worn with care, that we must make peace
in this land, and give it time to flower.
Our politics have grown so rancorous
that factions may soon turn on each other,
using weapons, not words, as arbiters.
In the hallowed halls of our government,
our nobles no longer debate issues
in lofty, patriotic cadences,
but instead use guttural invective
in attacking their opponents' good names.
Thus are the people's pressing needs ignored,
while hypocrites dispense moral judgments.

Oh, that this acrimony would abate,
and signs of hope would permit me to quote
my great predecessor, sad Abraham,
who, on the eve of his martyrdom, said:
'No more will native blood drench native soil.
No more will American soldiers set
flaming torches to American fields.
No more will pounding hooves of steeds of war
bruise our green meadows and muddy our streams.
Kindred, friends, and allies, who, in fury,
had butchered each other like animals,
will now, with smiles, march forward together.
The sharp edge of war, like an unsheathed knife,
will no more gash the flesh of its master.'
God give me the strength in these caustic times
that Abraham showed in his time of trial.

> *[ENTER JAMES OF HOUSTON]*

Good Lord James, share with us your recent news.

James. I bear an unhappy message, my liege.
The domestic tranquility you seek
still eludes us; the realm is in turmoil.
William of Clinton criticizes you,
and openly courts the common people.
He is familiar and pleasant with them,
and his words seduce their gullible hearts.
He tosses his hats into cheering crowds,
and smiles sweetly at women old and young.

Sire, the demagogue upstart eyes your throne!
He would seize the nobles' wealth for the mob.
He tells the rabble he will give them gold.
He would deflower maidens by the score.

George I. He is a menace indeed; tell me more.

James. Some of your key supporters now spurn you.
When like ladders they raised you to your throne,
you promised you would not raise their taxes.
But you did so – treacherously, they say –
in league with their profligate enemies.
These one-time partners now bear you ill will.

Other seeming friends also mean you harm.
One is John, the Scot from Arizona.
John is a brave and gallant war hero,
who also bears the scars of a martyr.
In the coming struggle for succession,
he could become a rival to your son.
As a soldier, John spent many bloody
hours crossing swords with strong adversaries.
At the end of one fateful battle, though,
his fellow Americans fled the scene,
leaving him alone, wounded, to be seized.
His captors would take no ransom for him,
so none of his many friends could save him.
The demons tortured John for five long years,

insisting that he curse his native land.
But he never gave in to their demands,
instead enduring the pain they dispensed.
When the barbarians freed him at last,
the people at home welcomed him with love.
Some said he should be President one day.
We must keep careful watch of this young John.
Still, Clinton is the more imminent threat.

George I.   Your description of John makes me feel sad,
and rouses in me the sin of envy –
towards the father of such a fine son.
John is the very emblem of honor,
amongst a grove the very straightest tree.
My young George, in contrast, is a disgrace.
Riot and dishonor stain his thick brow.
Oh, my friends, if only it could be proved
that some nocturnal fairy had exchanged
our children from the cribs in which they lay,
giving me the boy from Arizona,
and John's unwitting sire, George from Texas.
Then I would have his John, and he my George.

Where is my wanton – does anyone know?
It has been three months since I saw him last.
He is like a plague hanging over me.
I pray to God, my lords, he might be found.
Inquire in Richmond, amongst the taverns;
for there, I am told, he daily cavorts
with some loose and unrestrained companions,
of the sort who thrive on fraud and deceit.

Colin.   My lord, I saw the prince two weeks ago,
and told him of these proceedings today.

George I.   And what did the delinquent have to say?

Colin.   He said he was heading to an alehouse,

and had an engagement he could not break.

George I. He is depraved indeed, yet still I try
to see some sparks of a better nature,
which I hope will emerge in later years.

Richard. And so you should, my liege, and so you should.
We shall find him for you, and bring him here.
                    [EXIT ALL]

Act I. Scene II.—Richmond. A Room in a Tavern.

*[ENTER PRINCE GEORGE AND SIR JOHN
PIKESTAFF]*

Jack. *[WAKING UP]* Now, Junior, what time of day is it, lad?
Is it dark outside or is it light yet?

Prince. Why do you care, old slob, what time it is?
Why the devil should you care in the least?
You have drunk so many gallons of ale,
that you could not stir from your drooping chair
even if you had honest work to do!

Jack. You're right: the precise time matters little.
I care only whether it's night or day;
for I practice my profession – stealing –
under the pale moon and the starry skies,
and try to avoid the hot burning sun
under which honest fools toil for pennies.

Prince. You never seem to have any money,
whether gained justly or without scruple.
The food and drink here are not free, you know.
Yet you leave it to me to pay the bills.
And I, in turn, look to my creditors,
who are growing impatient with my debts.

Jack. I wish I knew the remedy against
this regrettable affliction of mine,
by which my purse always spills its contents.
The disease, I fear, is incurable.
In any case, God bless your creditors,
who seek to bootlick the heir apparent.
Oh, to be a President in training!
How easy it must be to raise money!
Tell me, boy, when you take charge of this realm,
will you leave your father's gallows standing?
I say, don't, when your time comes, hang a thief.

Prince. No, you will.

Jack. Oh? Then I'll be a brave judge.

Prince. You misunderstand. You are no jurist,
but might make a good executioner,
and thus earn fees for killing your own friends.

Jack. Oh, I see now. Well, better them than me!
Lad, you've been a bad influence on me.
God forgive you for the harm you've done me!
Before I knew you, George, I was nothing.
But I have become one of the wicked.

Prince. Oh, I've set a bad example for you?
Why that's a laugh, you mass of putrid flesh.
I bet you've already planned your next crime,
without any help or input from me.

Jack. And so what? Stealing is my vocation.
It's not sin to work in one's vocation.
Theft, George, is what I do for a living.
I won't beg pardon for my chosen trade.
My only point was that, since I met you,
I've become even more of a villain.
Still, when you do become the President,
please include me in the spoils of office.

For my part, though, I have more pressing concerns:
I want to toss a whore into the sheets!
        [EXIT JACK]
Prince. I know you well, and will awhile uphold
the unyoked humor of your idleness.
Yet herein will I imitate the sun,
who does permit the base contagious clouds
to smother up his beauty from the world,
so that, when the time is right to shine through,

being wanted, he may be more wondered at.
So, when this loose behavior I throw off
by so much shall I exceed men's slight hopes;
and like bright metal on a sullen ground,
my reformation, obscuring my fault,
shall show more goodly, and attract more eyes,
than that which has no foil to set it off.
            [ENTER JACK]
Jack, why are you still here? I thought you left.

Jack.   Richard of Wyoming has just arrived.
I saw him coming as I was leaving,
and chose to remain to hear his business.
            [ENTER RICHARD OF WYOMING]
Prince.   Welcome, Richard. What is your will with me?

Richard.   I come bearing news from the President.
Your father bids you to come to his court.

Prince.   Did he say why? Are there pressing affairs?

Richard.   He faces political challenges,
and needs both of his sons, but mainly you,
to prepare for possible encounters
with William of Clinton and John the Scot.

Prince.   Is armed conflict with these men imminent?

Richard.   Clinton is slowly building momentum,
but must be crushed if peace is to prevail.
We should attack him before he's too strong.
John is young and may be biding his time.
He may be waiting for your father's death.
But you, more than anyone, should watch him;
he may well stand between you and power.
I also just learned that in New Hampshire
a propagandist contends for the crown.
His name is Patrick, a staunch Catholic.

He writes pamphlets decrying the current
state of popular values and culture,
which are rotten, he says, and getting worse.
In short, there are plenty of good reasons
for you to cease your constant revelry
and conduct yourself like the royal heir.

Prince.   I'll come to the court as soon as I can.
  [RICHARD NODS AND EXITS]
Jack, help me prepare to meet my father,
who, in grave tones, will surely question me
about the particulars of my life.
Pretend to be him; show me no mercy.

Jack.   Shall I? Why not? This chair shall be my throne,
this blade my scepter, this cushion my crown.

Prince.   What a miserable monarch you make!

Jack.   Son, you are a source of marvel to me.
You not only spend time in bad locales;
you are also poorly accompanied.
Why do my subjects point at you in scorn?
I speak to you not in drink but in tears,
not in pleasure but in disappointment,
not in words only, but in woes also;
yet there is one virtuous man whom I
have often noted in your company,
though I do not know the gentleman's name.

Prince.   What manner of man, if I may inquire?

Jack.   He's a portly man, with a cheerful look,
a pleasing eye, and a noble carriage,
about fifty – no sixty – years of age.
Oh, now I remember: his name is Jack.
If he is prone to lewd activities,
then I am no good judge of character;

for I see virtue in his looks, my son.
Keep him with you always; the rest, banish.

Prince. You do sound like an angry President!
Now stand in for me; I'll play my father.

Jack. Depose me so soon? I've just gained the throne.

Prince. Yes, indeed; you're now demoted to prince.

Jack. I cower as such in your grave presence.

Prince. Now, young George, my son, where do you come from?

Jack. My noble lord, I am in from Austin.

Prince. The complaints I hear of you are grievous.

Jack. God's blood, my lord, such reproaches are false.

Prince. You dare swear in my presence, graceless boy?
Henceforth never look on my face again.
You are madly carried away from grace.
There is a devil that haunts you, stalks you,
in the likeness of a heavy old man.
Why do you indulge that gray ruffian?
Wherein is he good, but in tasting wine?
Wherein resourceful, but in craftiness?
Wherein crafty, but in base villainy?
Wherein villainous, but in everything?
Wherein worthy, but in nothing at all?

Jack. I do not know what person you might mean.

Prince. That most villainous, abominable
misleader of the young, Sir John Pikestaff.

Jack. My lord, I know the man.

Prince. I know you do.

Jack. He is no worse a man than you or me.
That he is old, the greater the pity;
his white hairs bear witness to time's advance.
But I deny that he's a whoremaster.
If the love of food and drink be a fault,
God help the wicked! The righteous are few.
If to be old and merry be a sin,
then many an old host that I know is damned.
If to be rotund is be to be hated,
then Pharaoh's lean kind are to be cherished.
No, father, he has not been my downfall.
If you want to upgrade my entourage,
then banish my other friends, but not Jack,
not that kind, sweet, and most valiant old man.
Banish plump Jack, and banish all the world.

Prince. I do, I will. Excuse me; I must go.
[PRINCE EXITS; JACK STANDS SILENT AND THEN EXITS]

Act I. Scene III.—*Washington. A Room in the Palace*.

[ENTER PRESIDENT GEORGE I, THE PRINCE, AND LORDS]

George I.   My lords, please allow the Prince and myself
a few moments for private conference.
          [EXIT LORDS]
It seems that God will punish my misdeeds,
with you the instrument of his revenge!
What else but God's hard and punitive will
can explain your wretched behavior?

Prince.   Your Majesty, I wish I had reasons
to rebut every charge made against me.
But I am guilty of many mistakes,
the products of youthful indiscretion.
So please pardon me for what I have done.
In the future, I will seek to improve.

George I.   It is for God – not me – to pardon you!
You have thrown away your advantages
by spurning your responsibilities.
By your constant failures to come to court,
you have lost your place in the state council,
which is now filled by your younger brother.
You are almost an alien to the
hearts of the nobles who attend on me.
Hopes for your own Presidency are dashed;
all men prophetically predict your fall.
If, in my day, I had acted this way,
public opinion would have opposed me;
I would never have ascended the throne.
Had I been so lavish of my presence,
so common and hackneyed in men's eyes,
so stale and cheap to vulgar company,
I would still be an outcast to power.
I rose through an opposite strategy:
by being seldom seen, I could not stir

without causing wonder, like a comet!
Thus did I keep my image fresh and new.

I had previously watched from afar
while prior Presidents profaned their names,
and dimmed the luster of this proud office,
by surrounding themselves with foolish wits,
shallow jesters, and low celebrities.
In seeking to impress the peasantry,
these leaders became too common themselves,
glutting the public's appetite for them.
Thus, the people grew so sick and weary
of these crude, pandering politicians,
that they purged the hacks whenever they could.

These memories portend danger for you,
son, though you have not yet stood for power.
The multitude already tires of you,
so accustomed are they to seeing you
consort with the dregs of society.

Prince. Good lord and dear father, please forgive me.
Hereafter, I shall be more like my self.

George I. Son, for all the world, you are, at this hour,
like Michael the Greek from Massachusetts,
with whom I vied to become President.
He was hapless, while I knew how to win.
As I was then, our enemies are now.
William of Clinton stands ready to fight.
John of Arizona is a hero.
The crowds cheer these men of action and deeds.
Oh, by my scepter and my soul to boot,
John has a stronger claim to rule than you,
though you bear my family crest and name.
However strong or weak his pedigree,
he knows the terrain of the battlefield.
And what undying honor he has gained

by beating opponents of great repute!
John has not only defeated such men;
but he has set them free without ransom,
making them his loyal and trusted friends.
Now, they threaten to combine against us,
and shake the peace and safety of our throne.
But why should I share this bad news with you?
Why, George, should I tell you about my foes –
you, my nearest and dearest enemy?

Prince.   Do not think so; you shall not find it so;
and God forgive them who so much have swayed
Your Majesty's good thoughts away from me!
I will redeem all my sins on John's head,
and at the end of some future battle,
be bold to tell you that I am your son.
Then I will wear a garment all of blood,
my face hidden behind a crimson mask,
which, when washed, will scour off my shame with it.
On the day of that struggle for power,
this same soldier of honor and renown,
this gallant John, this all-praised, sturdy knight,
and your unvalued George will chance to meet.
Then will I alter the score between us.
As of today, his deeds far exceed mine.
But John will be the means of my penance.
This, in the name of God, I promise here.
If, sire, I do perform this solemn vow,
I hope to regain your love and favor.
If I fail, my death will cancel our bond.
But I will die a hundred thousand deaths
before breaking this sacred pledge to you.

George I.   A hundred thousand rebels die in this.
I shall put you in charge of your own troops.
              [ENTER JAMES OF HOUSTON]
What is it, Lord James? You seem out of breath.

James.   My news, my liege, will admit no delay.
In Iowa and snowy New Hampshire
the fires of sedition are burning bright.
With his angry, pitchfork-wielding peasants,
Patrick the Pundit turns your friends on you,
while William of Clinton inflames your foes,
though Arizona John, for now, stands mute.
We must put down the mob led by Patrick,
and hope that, when we are done, our forces
can still beat William in a bid for power.

But even if we trounce Patrick quickly,
we face another revolt in Texas,
where your erstwhile ally Ross of Perot
accuses you of gross incompetence.
The rich pipsqueak will chirp in defiance
until a sword pierces his faithless heart.

George I.   James, we will not shrink from these challenges,
but rather address them one at a time.
First, we must quell the riots that Patrick
has roused against our royal majesty.
My younger son Jeb, from warm Florida,
will leave tomorrow for cold New Hampshire.
Next Wednesday, son George, you shall head there, too.
I will join you all shortly thereafter.
George, take with you Richard of Wyoming,
my minister with the love of power,
who hates dissent even more than I do.
With our great strength, we will crush the rebels,
and force the vile Patrick to kiss our ring.
We must spare his hateful head, however,
to regain the loyalty of his throng,
whose backing we will need against William.

Ross of Perot, though, will not fall quickly:
with his gold, he can mount a long campaign.
We may have to fight a war on two fronts:

with William and his swinish followers,
and with Ross and his cult of competence.
John, it seems, will stand aside from this strife,
waiting until he's strong enough to strike,
which may be years from now, when you, my son,
are ready for the throne in your own right.

    [EXIT ALL]

Act II. Scene I. – An Inn in New Hampshire.

Jeffrey.   My lord, the President, with his two sons
and thirty thousand plunder-loving troops,
stand ready for battle outside the town.
Their emissary, Lord James of Houston,
is here with a message from his master.
Shall we speak to him or send him away?

Patrick.   Maybe we can stall him for a short time,
until our expected guest has arrived.
Let us not confer with the man until
our religious ally Bishop Gerald,
a pious man of God, is at my side.
With him near, I appear to be stronger,
and James will take me more seriously.
Gerald also brings forces to my cause.
His credulous flocks are my best weapon
in my struggle to save this nation's soul.
Our preacher captain can inspire his men
in ways that I, as a layman, cannot.
           [ENTER GERALD, BISHOP OF LYNCHBURG]
Welcome, Bishop; I am glad to see you.
You come at a moment of decision.
The President, with thirty thousand men,
threatens this fearful town with fire and sword.
One of his aides is here to discuss terms.

Gerald.   What terms? Are we prepared to surrender?
I would rather die. Let's fight him tonight!

Patrick.   Though our cause is just and honorable,
yet we must be smart as we pursue it.
We are greatly outnumbered on the field,
and must consider whether here and now
are the proper place and time to engage.

Thus, we should hear from Lord James of Houston
before making any rash decisions.

Gerald. Call him in, then. I will listen to him.
> [EXIT JEFFREY]

I warn you: I will want to raise my sword
unless George gives us all that we demand.
> [ENTER JEFFREY AND JAMES OF HOUSTON]

James. If you will receive me with courtesy,
I will make you gracious offers of peace.

Patrick. Welcome, Lord James. We will hear you fairly.

James. Then let me proceed to my business.
The President has sent me to learn the
nature of your objections to his rule.
He asks why, with such bold hostility,
you have conjured such audacious cruelty
from the quiet breast of his civil peace.
In gratitude for your many good deeds,
however, he bids you name your complaints;
and with all speed, he will grant your desires.

Gerald. The President is kind; and we know well
his sense of when to promise, when to pay.
Why, my supporters and I gave him the
royalty he wears with such vanity!
We took up his cause, and protected him,
when he had only a few adherents,
and was held in low esteem by the world.
We raised funds for him, when others would not.
We told our friends and neighbors to help him.
We did so because we liked his values,
at least as he described them to us then.
He was, he said, a true conservative.
He would never, ever, increase taxes.
He denounced godless intellectuals.
Thus, with our help, he became President.
Yet he has betrayed his base of support!

James.   Tut, I did not come to listen to this.

Gerald.   Then to the point. He broke oath upon oath,
and committed wrong upon dreadful wrong.
He rules with a kind of moderation
at odds with our orthodox agenda.
This was not the bargain we made with him!
He cannot use our labor, our treasure,
and our hearts in this dishonest manner.
We have no choice but to resort to arms.

James.   Is this the message you want to convey?

Patrick.   Not so, Lord James. We will withdraw awhile,
and will provide our response at first dawn.

James.   I wish you would accept his kind offer.

Patrick.   Perhaps we will do so.

James.   Pray God you do.

Gerald.   Why should we trust this cunning President?
He has forced us to compel this offer,
which proceeds from policy, not from love.

James.   Foul traitor, you are wrong to take it so.
This offer comes from mercy, not from fear!

Patrick.   Then take, my good Lord, this memorandum,
which recites our general grievances.

James.   I will show this to my master, so that
we can meet in sight of both our armies
and either decide on peace, God willing,
or call on our swords to break the impasse.

Patrick. We will confer, my lord. Farewell to you.
　　　　[EXIT JAMES]
How should we respond to this olive branch?
Should we accept some sort of compromise,
or should we hold out for our full program?

Gerald. We have plenty of reasons to distrust
the President's offer of amnesty.
He will grant us our every desire
without inflicting any punishments?
I can't believe it, I don't believe it.
He will seek revenge when the time is right.

Jeffrey. Bishop, you are far too pessimistic.
If we reach a settlement acceptable
to our followers and the President,
our peace shall stand as firm as stone mountains.

Gerald. You are dangerously naïve, my friend.
If we reconcile with the President,
he may feign friendship and love toward us,
but he will remember our recent sins
until death dissolves all his memories.

Jeffrey. No, my lord, you are sadly mistaken.
This President, surrounded by troubles,
has not the luxury to hold grudges
against his friends for trifling grievances.
Besides, George has few rods left to brandish
against new offenders such as ourselves;
for earlier clashes have weakened him,
and he must husband his remaining strength
for the likes of Clinton and shrill Perot.
He will therefore wipe all his tables clean
and blot out his memory of our sins.

Gerald. I fear that you are very, very wrong.

Patrick. I've heard enough to make a decision.
True, the President may never love us;
he may even be suspicious of us;
but I doubt that he would cut off our heads.
We can surely wrest concessions from him,
and walk away with more than we have now.
The wanton, godless, cowardly Clinton,
whose wife is a witch schooled in the black arts,
portends an even greater disaster
than George receiving a renewed mandate.
We must join forces with the President
in readiness for the combat to come.

Gerald. I know it's wrong to bow to the tyrant;
were I the general here, we would fight!
But I yield to your authority,
as you are our leader, at least this year.
I'll save my hot sword of divine vengeance
for the womanish William of Clinton.

   [EXIT ALL]

Act II, Scene II.—The President's Camp, New Hampshire.

*[ENTER GEORGE I, JAMES OF HOUSTON,
THE PRINCE, JEB OF FLORIDA, AND RICHARD
OF WYOMING]*

George I.   The rebels' memorandum of complaints
offends my imperial majesty!   *[THROWS DOWN PAPER]*
How dare these traitors issue such demands?
My blood has been too cold and temperate.
Until now, out of respect for the Church,
I have calmly ignored indignities
perpetrated by her staunch defenders.
They have thus boldly trod on my patience,
thinking me smooth as oil, soft as young down.
I therefore lost that title of respect
that the proud never pay but to the proud.
But I am resolved to be more myself,
mighty and to be feared by everyone!

Good James, my dear friend and trusted counsel,
please share with me your thoughtful opinions.

James.   Dread sovereign, may I be frank with you?

George I.   Do not fear; this is not the Turkish court.
I am no tyrant who kills messengers.

James.   I would not recommend a massacre.
Radical surgery is not required.
Our body politic is distempered,
but may be restored to its former strength.
With good advice and little medicine,
Patrick and his minions will soon be cooled.
We need their help against a common foe:
William of Clinton, who would steal our wealth.

George I.   How fickle and changeable men can be.
It has been four short winters since Ronald

handed me the reins of royal power.
In those happy times, he and I broke bread
with this man of God who now threatens us.
James, I remember your warning back then
that his zealots might one day oppose me.
As you prophesied, grim necessity
would force me to deal with the liberals,
who would strike my left flank if not appeased.
One cannot govern, you explained to me,
without yielding some ground on some issues.
Yet pundit Patrick, who fights with paper,
though now, like a knight, he puts on armor,
thunders that I have disowned religion,
so that he should seize my scepter from me.
You warned that, having helped me to the throne,
his faction might later seek my downfall
if in some way I disappointed them.
These halfwits fail to see that their demands
only strengthen the hands of vile Clinton.
The educated and cultured elites
all consider Patrick an extremist.
They might back oily Clinton over me
if I am too generous with Patrick.
Clinton is smart and ambitious enough
to toss his angry rabble to the side,
in favor of these prosperous blue bloods,
when the moment is right for him to move.
His fervor for the poorest among us
will soon give way to his lust for power.

James.   Please, your grace, go to bed and get some sleep.
Your majesty has been feeling unwell.
Resolve to make peace tomorrow, then sleep.

George I.   I will take your counsel, which shows wisdom.
It would be foolish to shed these men's blood,
or, worse still, to estrange their followers.
They do not know it, but I am their friend.

With them, we will beat Clinton and Perot.

Richard.   Sire, could I offer one last suggestion?

George.   Yes, tell us.

Richard.   Let's arrest them anyway.
> *[GEORGE LOOK PUZZLED, EXITS; ALL OTHERS EXIT]*

> *[ENTER KING GEORGE, THE PRINCE, JEB OF*
> *FLORIDA, JAMES OF HOUSTON, RICHARD OF*
> *WYOMING, AND OTHERS]*

George I.   With an accord today, we are winners.
But still I must be stern with these traitors.
> *[TRUMPET SOUNDS; ENTER PATRICK THE*
> *PUNDIT, JEFFREY THE MANAGER, AND BISHOP*
> *GERALD]*

How now, my noble lords! It is not well
that you and I should meet upon such terms
as we now meet. You have deceived our trust,
and made us shed our easy robes of peace,
to crush our old limbs in ungentle steel.
This is not well, my lords; this is not well.
What can you damned rebels say for yourselves?

Patrick.   What I have done my safety urged me to.
We have no desire to cross swords with you
unless you leave us no other option.

George I.   Whenever have we denied your appeals?
Wherein, specifically, have we galled you?

Patrick.   We gave our list of laments to Lord James
and are prepared to discuss the details.

George I.   These complaints, indeed, you have publicized –
proclaimed in markets and read in churches –
all to give the garment of rebellion
some pretty colors that may please the eyes.
Never yet did shameful insurrection
lack such water colors to paint its cause.

Gerald.   For my own part, I could be well content
to entertain the last days of my life
with quiet hours; for I do protest

I have not sought out this day of conflict.

George I.   You have not sought it! How did it come, then?

Richard.   Rebellion lay in his way; he found it.

George I.   Gerald, I am appalled to see you here.
You are supposed to be a man of God!
One of your calling should not take up arms.
Rebellions are the work of ragged crowds
led by bellicose youths dressed in tatters.
With your rank and prestige, you have wrongly
blessed a base and bloody insurrection.
Tell me why, reverend lord, you did it.
How could you translate the holy gospels
into the harsh, boisterous tongue of war,
turning you books to graves, your ink to blood,
your pens to lances and your tongue divine
into an instrument of violence?
My lord Bishop Gerald, you showed better
when your congregants, convened by the bell,
encircled you to hear with devotion
your expositions on the sacred texts.
And yet here you are, encased in iron,
cheering a horde of rebels with your drum,
turning the word to sword and life to death.

Gerald.   I will answer for all of us churchmen.
Why have we taken up arms against you?
So the question stands. Briefly, this is why:
We are all diseased, this entire realm;
and with our licentious, promiscuous
conduct we are suffering so burning
hot a fever that we must bleed for it.
The sinful nature of this time forced us
to embrace this monstrous, contentious form.
I have in equal balance justly weighed
what wrongs our arms may do, what wrongs we bear,

and find our woes worse than our offenses.
As you said, we have not cloaked our complaints,
but rather have put them into writing.
Yet until we assembled an army,
we never obtained a royal hearing,
but were turned away by your courtiers.
The dangers of these recent restless days
have put us in these ill-beseeming arms
not to break peace or any branch of it,
but to establish here a peace indeed.
With the grant of our most just desires,
we will, with true, complete obedience,
stoop tamely to the foot of majesty.

George I.   We have, of course, reviewed your articles,
as Lord James told you yesterday we would.
We like them all, and do allow them well.
I swear here, by the honor of my blood,
that you have mistaken our purposes.
My lords, these grievances shall be redressed.
Upon my soul, they shall. If this please you,
then discharge your armies; let them go now,
as we will ours; and here between the troops
let's drink together friendly and embrace,
that all their eyes may bear home the image
of our restored affection and concord.

Patrick.   I accept your word for these redresses.

George I.   I give it you, and will maintain my word:
and thereupon I drink unto your grace.
         *[AIDE HANDS GOBLETS TO PRINCIPALS AND
         FILLS THEM FROM PITCHER]*
Patrick.   Go, captain, and inform our army of
this news of peace: let them have pay, and part.
         [EXIT OFFICER]
[RAISES GOBLET]   To you, my noble Lord James of Houston.
         [SHOUTS WITHIN]
James.   The word of peace is rendered: hark, how they shout!

George I. Go let our army be discharged as well.
[LOOKS TO RICHARD, WHO EXITS]
But first, my good lord, if it pleases you,
let our trains march by us, so that we may
look on those who would have tried to kill us.

Patrick. Go to our soldiers, my good Lord Jeffrey,
and let them march by before they depart.
[EXIT JEFFREY; REENTER RICHARD]
George I. Richard, why is our army still standing?

Richard. The leaders, having charge from you to stand,
will not go off until they hear you speak.

George I. They know their duties; they are so well trained.
[REENTER JEFFREY]
Jeffrey. *[TO PATRICK]* My lord, our troops have dispersed already.

Richard. Good tidings, my Lord Patrick; for the which
I do arrest you now of high treason;
and you rebels – Jeffrey, Bishop Gerald –
of capitol treason I attach you.

Patrick. Are these actions just and honorable?!

Richard. Is your assembly so? Is your revolt?

Gerald. Will you thus profane your word of honor?!

George I. I never promised not to arrest you.
I merely agreed that I would redress
the grievances shown in your articles,
in which your own personal liberty
was not a distinct item in the list.
By my honor, my promise of redress
I will perform with a most Christian care.
But for you, rebels, look to taste what's due

to you for treachery and sedition!
[TURNS TO SOLDIERS]
Strike up our drums; pursue the scattered strays.
Richard, convey these traitors to prison,
where they will await our royal pleasure.
[EXIT RICHARD AND REBELS]
Thus ever did rebellion find rebuke.
We must decide how to dispose of them.
We could dismember them for spectacle;
the rabble loves drawing and quartering.
Or we could save them for our own uses.
We could compel them to sing our praises
in exchange for their freedom and support.

James. Patrick is too valuable to kill.
We need the pundit's oratory
to rally the riffraff against Clinton.
[GEORGE I NODS AND ALL EXIT]

SCENE.—America.

Act II. Scene IV.—Richmond. A Room in a Tavern.

> *[ENTER PRINCE GEORGE AND SIR JOHN PIKESTAFF]*

Prince.   By God, I am exceedingly weary,
though not from any heroic exploits.
My father's bloodless defeat of Patrick
spared me the task of vanquishing rebels.

Jack.   Has it come to that? I thought weariness
dared not attach itself to the high-born.

Prince.   I'm afraid it does, though it discolors
my noble complexion to admit it.

Jack.   A prince should so guard his reputation
as never to display any weakness.

Prince.   Indeed, this need to tend to my 'image'
makes me fall out of love with my greatness.
I can be disgraced far too easily.
Perhaps I should never be seen with you.

Jack.   How ill it is you should talk so idly.
Tell me, how many princes would do so,
their fathers being so sick as yours is now?

Prince.   Not very many, old man, I dare say.
Dutiful sons should comfort their fathers.

Jack.   Nobody calls you a dutiful son!
When did the President start feeling bad?

Prince.   His stomach was making noises on the
eve of the confrontation with Patrick.
Last night, I hear, he vomited in the

lap of a Japanese dignitary,
and then lost consciousness altogether.
Some of his doctors predict he will die;
others say he will fully recover.

Jack. And do you have a preference, my boy?

Prince. May I be frank with you?

Jack. Yes, certainly.

Prince. I tell you, it is not fit that I should
seem sad over my father's affliction –
though I can tell you, as a kind of friend,
that in truth I am very sad indeed.

Jack. Surely the thought of ascending the throne
helps mitigate at least some of your woe.

Prince. By this hand, you think me as far in the
Devil's book as you are, Sir John Pikestaff!
I must tell you, honestly: my heart bleeds
inwardly that my father is so sick,
but keeping such vile company as you
precludes a proper showing of sorrow.
What would you think of me if I should weep?

Jack. I would think you a princely hypocrite.

Prince. Exactly! It would be every man's thought.
And what about me would make them think so?

Jack. Why, the fact that you've been lewd and debauched.

Prince. But I should not balk from fear of rebuke.
I will go to my father in private.
The gossiping chatterers need not know.   *[BOTH EXIT]*

Act II. Scene V.— Washington.   The Palace.

[ENTER KING GEORGE I IN HIS NIGHTGOWN]

George I.   How many thousands of my poor subjects
are at this hour asleep! Oh gentle sleep,
Nature's soft nurse, how have I frightened you,
that you no more will weigh my eyelids down
and steep my senses in forgetfulness?
Why do you visit peasants' shabby huts
but scorn the perfumed chambers of the great?
Oh, you fortunate ruffians, lie down!
Uneasy lies the head that wears a crown.
                [LIGHT KNOCK ON DOOR]
Who's there? I'm still awake. You may enter.
                [ENTER JAMES OF HOUSTON AND JEB OF
                FLORIDA]
James, friend, are you, like me, wakeful with care?
Jeb, my son, what a surprise to see you!
Why are you not asleep at this late hour?

Jeb.   We saw shafts of light from under your door,
and decided to see how you're feeling.

George I.   Jeb, where is your older brother, Prince George?

James.   I think he's gone to hunt wild boar, my lord.

George I.   Jeb, why aren't you with the Prince, your brother?
He loves you, son, but you do neglect him.
You stand higher in George's affection
than all your siblings. Cherish it, my boy;
and after I'm dead, you can mediate
between him and others in our household.

Jeb.   I shall observe him with all care and love.

George I.   Why are you not with him hunting wild boars?

Jeb.   He's not hunting, but dining in Richmond.

George I.   And how accompanied? Can you tell that?

Jeb.   With Pikestaff and his other followers.

George I.   The richest soil is most subject to weeds;
and he, the noble image of my youth,
is overspread with them: therefore my grief
stretches itself beyond the hour of death.
The blood weeps from my heart when I conceive
the rotten times that you shall look upon
when I am sleeping with my ancestors.
For when his headstrong riot has no curb,
and rage and hot blood are his counselors,
oh, with what swift wings will he fly towards
hostility, peril, and destruction!

James.   Perhaps, my lord, you misunderstand him.
         [LIGHT KNOCK ON DOOR]
George I.   Who else can this be at this absurd hour?
         [ENTER RICHARD OF WYOMING]
Richard.   I beg pardon, my liege; I heard voices,
and saw light, emanating from this room.
I thought you might be pleased to hear good news,
since you happened to rise early this morn.

George I.   I'm not up early; I never did sleep.
Although I'm ill, my cares make me fitful.

Richard.   I apologize; I'll return later.

George I.   Never mind; you're here now. What's your message?

Richard.   Thank you, sire; I wish you recovered health,
and hope my tidings bring new happiness.
With threats of abuse and appeals to greed,
we have persuaded Patrick the Pundit

to use his shrill tongue to advance your cause.
With him stoking the embers of hatred
that smolder in the hearts of the rabble,
we will blunt the appeal of vile Clinton,
who would steal – and redistribute – our wealth.
With envy and rage clouding their judgment,
the poor will reject their true champion.
And we will renew our hold on power.

George I. *[COUGHING]*
Why should this good news make me feel sicker?
Will Fortune never come with both hands full,
but instead write fair words in foul letters?
She either gives a stomach but no food
or else a feast but no stomach for it.
Thus may a peasant be blessed with good health
while a nobleman is cursed with disease.
I should rejoice now at this happy news,
but lack the strength to enjoy the bounty.
My sight fails me, and my brain is giddy.
Please, come and help me; for I am much ill.
Though all night I begged sleep to visit me,
now she comes upon me too suddenly.
          [THE PRESIDENT LOSES CONSCIOUSNESS]
James. Comfort, your highness!

Jeb. Oh, royal father!

James. Be patient, princes; these fits, as you know,
are with his lordship quite ordinary.
Stand from him, give him air; he'll soon be well.

Jeb. No, no; he cannot long endure these pangs.
          [PRESIDENT OPENS HIS EYES]
George I. I pray you, lift me up into my bed.
I lack strength to think on affairs of state.
Let there be no noise made, my gentle friends.

Set down the crown upon my pillow here.
[PRESIDENT LOSES CONSCIOUSNESS]
Jeb.   His eye is hollow, and he changes much.
[ENTER PRINCE GEORGE]
Prince.   How fares the President?

Jeb.   Very poorly.

James.   Not so much noise, my lords. Sweet prince, speak low;
your royal father is disposed to sleep.

Jeb.   Let us withdraw into the other room.

James.   *[TURNING TO THE PRINCE]*
Will it please you to go along with us?

Prince.   No, I will sit here with the President.
*[EXIT ALL BUT THE PRINCE AND SLEEPING
PRESIDENT]*
Why does the crown lie there on his pillow,
being so troublesome a bedfellow?
Oh golden care that deprives royal eyes
of slumber on many a wakeful night.

Look at that downy feather near his mouth.
Why does it not stir, even a little?
If my father is breathing, it should move.
*[PRINCE LISTENS CAREFULLY FOR BREATHING
BUT HEARS NONE]*
Oh, my gracious lord! My dearest father!
This sleep is sound indeed; this is a sleep
that has silenced too many Presidents.
Oh, my liege, why have you forsaken me?
Must I, alone, take up your cares of state?
Your due from me are these tears of sorrow,
which nature and filial tenderness
shall pay you plenteously, dear father.
My due from you is this resplendent crown,
which I, as your oldest son, inherit.

[PRINCE PLACES THE CROWN ON HIS HEAD]
Lo, here it sits, where Heaven shall guard it;
and all the strength in the world shall not take
this honor from me, until I pass it
to my own child, as you left it to me.
        [PRINCE EXITS WEARING CROWN]

George I. *[WAKING]* Jeb! Lord James!
        [RE-ENTER JAMES OF HOUSTON, JEB, AND
        RICHARD OF WYOMING]
James. Does Your Majesty need us?

George I. Why did you leave me here alone, my lords?

Jeb. We left the prince my brother here, my liege,
who undertook to sit and watch by you.

George I. Where is he? Let me see him; he's not here.

James. This door is open; he has gone this way.

Jeb. He didn't come through the room where we stayed.

George I. Where's the crown? Who took it from my pillow?

James. When we withdrew, my liege, we left it here.

George I. The Prince has taken it; go, seek him out.
Is he so hasty that he supposes
my sleep my death? Find him, James; chide him here.
        [EXIT JAMES OF HOUSTON]
This deed of his conjoins with my disease,
and helps to end me. See what things sons are!
How quickly nature falls into revolt
when glittering gold becomes her object!
For this, foolish, over-careful fathers
have broken their sleep with anxiety,
their brains with care, their bones with industry.
For this, they have piled up, with great effort,

heaps of riches hard-earned and hard-maintained.
For this, they have been thoughtful to invest
their sons with arts and military skills.
When, like bees, we cull from every flower
its virtuous sweets, our legs packed with wax,
our mouths with honey, we bring it back home,
to our hive, and are murdered for our pains!
Such are the rewards of loving fathers.

[RE-ENTER JAMES]
Where is he who will not stay long enough
to let sickness, his friend, finish me off?

James. My lord, I found the Prince in the next room,
washing with kindly tears his gentle cheeks.
See, he is coming back to comfort you.

George I. Tell me, why did he take away the crown?
[RE-ENTER THE PRINCE]
Oh look, here he is. Come here to me, George.
Depart the chamber, leave us here alone.
*[EXIT JAMES AND THE REST BUT THE PRINCE
AND PRESIDENT]*
Prince. I never thought to hear you speak again.

George I. Your wish, my son, was father to that thought.
I stay too long by you. I weary you.
Do you so hunger for my empty chair
that you would seize my honors for your own
before your hour is ripe? Oh, foolish youth,
you seek greatness that will overwhelm you.
Wait but a little: the winds holding up
the clouds of my dignity are so weak
that they will quickly drop. My day is dim.
You've stolen something that, in a few hours,
would have become your own without offense.
You have confirmed my worst expectations.
The way you live shows you do not love me,
and you would have me die assured of it.
You hid a thousand daggers in your thoughts,

which you have whetted on your stony heart,
to stab at a mere half hour of my life.
What, you can't spare me even half an hour?
Then leave me now and dig my grave yourself,
and ring cathedral bells to signify
not that I am dead, but that you are crowned.
Let all the tears that should bedew my hearse
be drops of balm to sanctify your head.
Only cover me with forgotten dust;
give to the worms, him who gave you your life.
Pluck down my officers, break my decrees;
for now a time is come to mock at form.
George the Second is crowned! Up, vanity!
Down, royal state! Sage counselors, depart!
And to the royal court assemble now,
from every region, apes of idleness!
Now should each State purge itself of its scum.
Do you have a ruffian who swears, drinks,
revels the night, robs, murders, and commits
the oldest sins the newest kind of ways?
Be happy, he will trouble you no more!
America will not punish his crimes,
but rather will give him office and might.
The second George will loosen the muzzle
that curbs the appetites of the wild dog,
whose fangs crave the flesh of the innocent.
Oh, my poor country, sick with civil blows,
if my firm rule could not maintain order,
what will you do when ruled by rioters?
Oh, you will be a wilderness again,
peopled with wolves, your old inhabitants.

Prince. Pardon me, my liege; if not for my tears –
moist impediments to the art of speech –
I would have begged you to halt this rebuke,
before you had vented so much anger,
and I had felt the full fury of it.

There is your crown. Let the ruler who wears
the crown immortal long guard it for you.
If I love that band more than your honor,
let me never again rise from my knees,
but always remain prostrate before you,
as I now am in dutiful spirit.
As God is my witness, when I came in,
and found no trace of breath in your highness,
how cold it struck my heart! If I do feign
this humility, then let me die now,
and be remembered for rash wantonness,
and never live to show the doubtful world
the noble changes I intend to make.
Coming to look on you, thinking you dead,
and feeling almost dead inside myself,
I spoke to the crown as if it had sense,
and upbraided it for its wrongs to you.
'You've fed on my father's body,' I said.
Accusing it, I put it on my head,
to confront it, as with an enemy
who had before my face killed my father.
But if it did infect my blood with joy,
or swell my thoughts to any strain of pride;
if I felt even a spark of gladness
at the thought of the sheer might behind it,
let God forever keep it from my head,
and make me like the penniless vassal,
who must with awe and terror kneel to it!

George I. Oh my son! This crown is our common foe.
God put it in your mind to take it hence,
that you might win the more your father's love,
pleading so wisely in excuse of it.
Come here, George; sit yourself down by my bed,
and hear what might be my final advice.
God knows by what dark means I won this crown.

I know how hardly it sits on my head.
To you it shall descend more quietly,
with greater perceived legitimacy;
for the soil of starting a dynasty
follows the founder into the cold earth.
In my deft hands, the crown was an honor
snatched boisterously from men with stronger claims.
And those who helped me kept reminding me
that I gained power through their assistance.
These allies grew haughty and quarrelsome.
I've had to endure their endless complaints
through all the years of my turbulent reign.
But now my death, if it comes, will change things;
for what I gained through toil and exertion
will be passed to you as though it's your due.
Yet, though your legs will stand firmer than mine,
you will still need to strengthen your power.
Grievances against me will remain fresh.
My friends' stings and teeth are newly removed.
Their wounds still smart, and they still plot vengeance.
You must befriend these seething discontents.
It should therefore be your policy, son,
to busy giddy minds with foreign strife;
so that wealth and fame earned in wars abroad
will make them forget their disputes with us.
I would say more, but my lungs are so weak
that strength of speech is wholly denied me.
How I came by the crown, Oh God forgive,
and grant it may with you in true peace live.

Prince.   You won it, wore it, and gave it to me;
then plain and right my possession must be.
And I will maintain that right against all.
> *[PRESIDENT LOSES CONSCIOUSNESS; PRINCE*
> *OPENS THE DOOR TO CHAMBER]*
Brother, Lord James, Richard: he sleeps again.
> *[EXIT PRINCE]*
Jeb.   Oh God, let him live. We are not ready.
I fear that Clinton is too strong to thwart.

My poor father's mind dwells in fantasy;
our succession is far from guaranteed.

[EXIT ALL]

Act III. —*The Streets of Washington.*

[*ENTER CHORUS*]

Chorus.   Ladies and gentlemen, please excuse me.
I must intrude, at this point in our play,
to share with you some key information.
In the next scene, our players will transport
you many fateful months forward in time.
President George's health has much improved,
though he remains too frail to fight in war.
Yet his sons, learning of troubles abroad,
have carried their swords to distant countries.
George slashed through the jungles of Panama
to seize a venal upstart general,
while Jeb, with a powerful armada,
sailed to Kuwait to check an invasion.
Though these sons, through their valor, earned glory,
they left their father without protection,
and thus vulnerable to an armed mob.
Still, when messengers told them of danger,
these sons, in great haste, departed for home.
> *[EXIT CHORUS; ENTER WILLIAM OF CLINTON, A*
> *MERCHANT, AND A COMPANY OF MUTINOUS*
> *CITIZENS WITH STAVES, CLUBS, AND OTHER*
> *WEAPONS]*

Clinton.   Before we proceed further, hear me speak.

All.   Speak, speak!!

Clinton.   You'd rather die fighting than starve?

All.   Yes!

Clinton.   Who is the people's worst enemy?

All.   President George! He has forgotten us!

Clinton.   What should we do to him?

All.   We should kill him!

Clinton.   We need not kill him, but must depose him.
Then we will set the price of food and drink!
Then will the rich, whom the President serves,
surrender some of their booty to us.
Is this a plan? Will you all follow me?

All.   Let's stop talking about it and do it!

Merchant.   Hold on for a moment, good citizens!
Does the old man really deserve to fall?

Clinton.   You're right to call us the good citizens,
though the rich seize that title for themselves,
and call us poor souls stupid and lazy.
But tell me: if these nobles are so good,
why won't they share some of their wealth with us?
Though their sheds are piled high with wheat and corn,
they won't even throw us their table scraps.
Our very poverty indicts their rule:
if, as they claim, we shared in their success,
we would be strong, healthy, and literate.
But look at us: we scavenge like mad dogs!
Let's terminate these cruelties with our pikes,
before privation makes us thin as rakes.
God knows I speak this in hunger for bread,
and not in hatred and thirst for revenge.

Angry Citizen.   I'm hungry, too, but I still want revenge!
George must die. We should assassinate him!
But why only him? He's part of a class.
Why not murder and mutilate them all?
They all fatten themselves on our labor!

Merchant.   Or better yet, why not let them all live?
If you are mad dogs, as your leader claims,

you may get to taste blood from your victims,
but you'll end up dead, lying in a ditch.
The rich always prevail; you all know it.
So, go speak calmly with the President.
Appeal to his kind, generous nature.
Show him the deference that he deserves,
as one who served this country valiantly.
When still a lad of just seventeen years,
he fought courageously in war at sea.
Though now he is old and weak from illness,
he remains supreme Commander in Chief.
He will see the wisdom of helping you.

Clinton.   I acknowledge his valor in battle,
and I honor his youthful sacrifice;
but in his dotage, he has grown too proud.
He tells us we deserve our misfortunes.
He treats us with contempt, calls us cowards.
He calls me a traitor to my country
for opposing, while young, a tragic war
the wisest chroniclers now say was wrong.
He assails me further because, while young,
I smoked a seductive weed with my friends,
though, unlike my peers, I did not inhale.
Are these reasons to let throngs go hungry?
These are diversions to change the subject!
            [SHOUTS]
My friends, what shouts are these? Wait, who comes here?
            [ENTER JAMES OF HOUSTON]
Merchant.   Why, it's the worthy Lord James of Houston,
one who always loved the common people.

James.   My countrymen, what plot are you hatching?
Where are you going with those bats and clubs?
What is the matter? Tell me, I pray you.

Clinton.   Our business is not unknown to your liege.
For two weeks we've made our intentions clear.

We will now with actions make good our threats.

James. My friends and neighbors, why undo yourselves?
Why strike your royal father, who loves you?

Clinton. Sir, we cannot further undo ourselves;
we are already completely undone.

James. I tell you, friends, the nobility takes
most charitable care of your people.
You can't blame the President for famine,
or for the hunger pangs in your stomachs.
You would better shake your staves at heaven
than raise them against your fair President.
God, in his anger, made the pestilence,
to punish the peasantry for its sins.
Blame yourselves, but not George, for your trials,
which will only get worse through more folly.
You slander your betters, who care for you
like fathers, when you call them enemies.

Clinton. Care for us?! Why, they've never cared for us.

James. The rich do the thinking and the planning
for the remainder of society.
Examine the ways in which your betters,
in governing this body politic,
carefully consider the greater good;
and you shall find that every benefit
you receive comes to you from their kind hands.
There is little you must do for yourselves,
save rise in the morning to earn your bread.

Do not follow this demagogue William!
He is here only for his own advantage,
and not to help the 'downtrodden masses.'
We know his type; he'll shed innocent blood
to gain personal power for himself.

He wants to impose his will on others.
To pursue these ends, he feigns compassion.
In justice, the President must crush him.
A household must exterminate its rats.

Clinton.   Today George lacks the means to work his will,
while I have the advantage of power
that can produce showers of noble blood!
Yet it's far from my mind that a crimson
tempest should bedrench the soil of this land.
Our demands are modest: we just want food.
> *[ENTER THE PRESIDENT AND RICHARD OF WYOMING]*

James.   Hail, President of the United States!
> *[TO HIMSELF UNDER HIS BREATH]*

Why does he come here unaccompanied
before his sons arrive to protect him?
His illness has affected his judgment.

George I.   What's the matter with you dissentious rogues?
Though your supporters wish you were lions,
they will find instead that you act like hares.
James, tell me what 'redress' they are seeking.

James.   They say the nobles have plenty of corn,
and should sell some to them at fair prices.

George I.   They say?! Hang them! How much they do presume!
They say there is grain enough?! Who asked them?

James.   *[QUIETLY TO THE PRESIDENT]*
There is no need here, Sire, for harsh measures.
These men are almost fully persuaded;
for though they lack wisdom and good judgment,
they are cowards and too timid to act.
And you recently have been very ill.
Your sons and their troops, returning from wars,
are still a day's ride from this lawless place.

George I. *[TO THE MOB]*
This rabble must first unroof this city
before it ever prevails over me.

Clinton. What makes you better than anyone else?
You landed barons, with your constant wars,
are no great stewards of our native land.
You have no talent or gift for wise rule.
You're too contemptuous of normal folks.
You're wrong to see no virtue in craftsmen,
to heap scorn on men with leather aprons.

Angry Citizen. This President does no real honest work,
and neither do his evil counselors.
Let the magistrates be laboring men,
and let us laborers rule the country!

Dick. That's right, my fellows! A calloused hand is
the best sign of a truly noble mind.

Clinton. Then seize the old man; take him prisoner.
*[MEMBERS OF THE MOB SEIZE AND HOLD
PRESIDENT GEORGE, ALONG WITH THE
MERCHANT, JAMES OF HOUSTON, AND RICHARD
OF WYOMING]*
Let my enemies all fall before me;
for I am inspired with the spirit of
putting down presidents and senators.
[TO DICK] Command silence!

Dick. Silence, our leader speaks!

Clinton. *[STARING AT GEORGE, JAMES, AND RICHARD]*
How now gentlemen? *[TURNING TO THE MOB]*
Why, look how they change!
Look at these tyrants, who moments ago
spoke without pity for the destitute.
[LOOKING AT GEORGE]
Do not dare – for shame – to talk of mercy,

for your reasoning against compassion,
which tells the luckless to accept their fates,
turns on you like a dog on his master.

> *[CLINTON SITS DOWN INTO CHAIR BROUGHT TO*
> *HIM BY PEOPLE IN CROWD]*

George I.   Sirrahs, look where the sturdy rebel sits,
in the chair of state: look how he aspires
to the crown and to reign as President.

James.   What, shall we suffer this? Let's pluck him down.
My heart burns with anger; I can't brook it.

George I.   Be patient, brave warrior from Houston.
Tomorrow my sons will arrive with troops.
This obscure and lowly rabble will not
dare to shed the sacred blood of our house.
It is impossible that I should die
by such miserable vassals as these.

Clinton.   Silence! Your heroic sons are not here.
The peasantry has risen up in arms,
and it burns with hate and revenging fire.
You men may not live to see the morrow.
Envision your heads atop the town gates!

> *[TURNING TO THE MOB]*

It is to you, good people, that I speak,
over whom, as of this moment, I reign;
for I am the rightful heir to the crown.
I was born of an honorable house.

Dick.   Villain, your father sold parts for used carts.

Clinton.   And Adam was a gardener. So what?
[GLARES AT DICK] I fear neither sword nor fire nor battle.
Be brave, comrades, for your captain is brave,
and vows to reform this corrupted land.

Angry Citizen.   What kinds of reforms? Will I benefit?

Clinton.   From now on, all three-dollar loaves of bread
shall be sold for only half a dollar;
> *[CHEERS]*

brewing weak beer shall be a felony;
> *[CHEERS]*

the pissing conduit shall carry wine;
> *[CHEERS]*

all property shall be held in common;
> *[CHEERS]*

and Wall Street shall become a grassy field!

Citizens.   God save your highness!

Clinton.   Thank you, good people.

Dick.   First thing we do is kill all the lawyers!   *[CHEERS]*

Clinton.   Yes, that I mean to do. Is it not wrong
that words on paper should undo a man?
I hate the silken knaves that make such words;
I intend to abolish all contracts;
I will burn all the records of the realm.
> *[CHEERS]*

From my mouth shall come the law of the land.
From this day on, there shall be no money.
Everyone will eat and drink on my tab,
> *[CHEERS]*

wear uniforms bearing my coat of arms,
and worship me as vassals must their lord.
> *[SPEAKS SOFTLY TO HIMSELF]*

The proudest rich man shall not wear a head
on his shoulders, lest he pay me tribute.
There shall not a maid be married, but she
shall pay to me first her virginity.
Men shall share their wives with me, as their lord.

Dick.   If we mean to thrive and do good, you must
break open the jails, free the prisoners!

George I.   You rebels, the filth and scum of this land,
who should be marked to hang from the gallows,
lay your weapons down; return to your homes.
If you disperse, I will be merciful;
but if you go forward with this revolt,
I'll be wrathful and inclined to spill blood.
Therefore yield, or die.

> *[LAUGHTER]*

Clinton.   You have no power.
You're an infirm, weak, and despised old man.

George.   I am amazed by this rebellion.
Not all the water in the rough rude sea
can wash the balm off an anointed head.
The breath of worldly men cannot depose
the deputy elected by the Lord.
I had thought myself lawful President.
And if I am, how dare your legs forget
to kneel before me in abject duty?
If I am not, show me the hand of God
that has dismissed me from my stewardship;
for well I know, no hand of blood and bone
can seize the sacred handle of my scepter,
unless he do profane, steal, or usurp.
Though I seem barren and bereft of friends,
yet know, my master, God omnipotent,
is mustering in his clouds, for my use,
armies of pestilence; and they shall strike
your children and grandchildren yet unborn.
For every man whom Clinton has pressed
to lift shrewd steel against our golden crown,
God for his George has in heavenly pay
a glorious angel. If angels fight,
weak men must fall, for heaven guards the right.
Your actions here are dangerous treason.

Clinton.   I do not obey; I was born to rule.

*[COMMOTION; A CLOAKED MAN FORCEFULLY
MOVES THROUGH THE CROWD TOWARDS
CLINTON AND THE PRESIDENT]*

What is all this noise? What is going on?
Ask this man his purpose, why he appears
in such a manner and at such a time.

Dick. *[TO THE MAN]*

What are you, rich or poor? What is your name?
*[MAN TAKES OFF HIS CLOAK, REVEALING
HIMSELF TO BE PRINCE GEORGE]*

Prince.   My name is George, rightful heir to the throne.
In my fervor to reach the President,
I've ridden a day ahead of my peers.
For my part, I may speak it to my shame,
I have been a truant to chivalry.
And so, before my father's majesty,
in order to save blood on either side,
I challenge Clinton to a single fight.
I'll prove my right in trial by battle.
Otherwise, many an innocent soul
shall pay full dearly for this encounter.

George I.   This gesture warms your father's heart with pride.
Son, I don't fear for you in such combat,
for God guides the arm of he who is right.
And yet infinite considerations
counsel against a clash of unequals.
You are a knight, while he is a coward.
There is no honor in slaying this foe.

Prince.   If high birth makes me too good a swordsman,
we can fight each other with our bare hands.
There is no shame in killing this traitor.
[TURNING TO CLINTON]
'Lord,' mark my greeting well; for what I say
[THROWS DOWN GAGE]
my body shall make good upon this earth,
or my soul answer for it in heaven.

Pale trembling coward, there I throw my gage,
disclaiming any advantage that my
blood of royal lineage might give me.
If guilty dread has left you so much strength
as to take up my honor's pawn, then stoop.
What my tongue speaks, my right drawn sword will prove.

Clinton.   Setting aside your high blood's royalty,
I do defy you, and I spit on you.
By all my hopes, most falsely do you lie.
Yet I will not stoop to take up your gage.
You are a handful; we are populous.
Of course you would offer single combat,
and wrap yourself in knighthood and honor.
I am not so stupid as to accept.
I'm immune to your appeals to honor.
I claim the scepter by right of conquest.
I mean to take possession of my right.
> *[NODS TO OTHERS WHO SEIZE ON AND HOLD
> PRINCE]*

Prince.   I should have known that you would spurn my gage.
Of course you have no concept of honor.
You're a cracker, a hick from Arkansas,
who would rule this land without dignity.
My brother will arrive a day from now
to settle scores with your dirty rabble.
If today you rashly kill the President,
it will make things worse for you tomorrow.

Clinton.   Let me drown these false hopes of yours in tears.
This morning, my ally Ross of Perot
intercepted and attacked your brother.
Having gathered flocks of friends to himself,
he battled noble Jeb to a standstill,
and now prevents him from rescuing you.
Perot intends to march on Washington
to ensure my succession to the throne.
So you must accept this new status quo:
Perot hates me, but despises you more.

George I.   So it is. The wheel has come full circle.
My presidency is lost forever.
The army of Perot has got the field,
and my son prevented from saving me.

Clinton.   Take off your crown, that you may keep your head.

George I.   *[TAKES OFF THE CROWN AND HOLDS IT BY
               HIS SIDE]*
I take off the crown, but give you my curse;
so that, when most you need comfort, you get
no more than I've received from your cruel hands.
Though the Prince's bravery touches me,
and I'd save the throne for him if I could,
I am surrounded by too many foes.
Great Hercules himself must yield to odds;
and many strokes, though with a little axe,
hew down and fell the hardest-timbered oak.
              [LOOKS AT THE PRINCE]
By many hands is your father subdued.
No matter. Of comfort, let no man speak.
Let no one wrong me with flattering tongues.
Let's talk of graves, of worms, and epitaphs;
make dust our paper and with rainy eyes
write sorrow on the bosom of the earth.
Let's choose executors and talk of wills;
and yet not so, for what can we bequeath
except our deposed bodies to the ground?
Our lands, our lives and all are Clinton's now.
And nothing can we call our own but death
and those small pieces of the barren earth
that one day will cover over our bones.
For God's sake, let us sit upon the ground
and tell tales of the deaths of presidents;
how some have been deposed; some slain in war,
some haunted by the ghosts they have deposed;
some poisoned by their wives; some sleeping killed.
All murdered: for within the hollow crown

that rounds the temples of a president
keeps death his court; and there the jester sits,
scoffing his state and grinning at his pomp.
Do not mock flesh and blood with reverence.
Throw away respect, tradition, and form;
for you have but mistook me all this while.
I live like you, feel want, taste grief, need friends.
How can you say I am a president?

Prince. *[TURNS TO THE CROWD]*
You misguided villains are all traitors
in following this usurping Clinton!

Clinton. What, should they follow you – a whoremonger?
They see in me their natural leader.
Thrones need not always pass to eldest sons.
May not a President adopt an heir?
If so, then I can become lawful lord.
Let your father freely give me his crown,
and thus avoid a worse calamity.
You are lucky, Prince, to still be alive.

George I. Victory is yours, Clinton, with no blows struck.
What you will have, I'll give, and willing too;
for do we must what force will have us do.

Clinton. Confirm the crown to me and to my heirs,
and you may spend your final years in peace.

George I. Yes. I am content: William of Clinton,
enjoy my office on this condition:
that you spare the lives of my two dear sons,
whom, of necessity, I must disown.
Banish them to save their lives if you must.

James. Sire, you have given away too much here,
and brought shame upon your noble blood line.
Are we to be governed by this dastard?

What a wrong is this to the Prince your son!
You have injured both him and the nation.
Surely he prefers death to dishonor.
     [ENTER QUEEN BARBARA]
Here comes the queen, whose looks show her anger.

George I.   Be patient, gentle queen; I had no choice
but to make an arrangement with Clinton.
To save our sons, I yielded up the throne.

Barbara.   Who can remain patient in such extremes?
Wretched man, I wish I had died a maid
and never seen you, never borne you sons,
you are so unnatural a father.
Have they deserved to lose their birthright thus?
Had you but loved them half so well as I,
or felt that pain that I did for them once,
or nourished them as I did with my blood,
you would have risked your cherished life for them
rather than name vile Clinton as your heir.

Prince.   Father, you cannot disinherit me.
If you reign now, why should I not succeed?
Thank you, Sire, for wanting to protect me,
but a life of shame is not worth living.
I've put my infamous days behind me,
and now seek to live a life of honor.

Clinton.   Honor again. You bluebloods amuse me.
Can't you see that honor has no real use?
Can honor set a leg or an arm? No.
Can it reduce the pain of a wound? No.
Does honor have skill in surgery? No.
What is honor? A word. What's in it? Air.
A trim reckoning! Who has this honor?
He who died last week. Does he feel it? No.
Does he hear it? No, it's inaudible.
It's perceptible only to the dead.

Why will it not reside with the living?
Because its luster can only abate.
I've therefore resolved to have none of it.
And you patricians should get over it.

George I.   Pardon me, my queen; pardon me, sweet son:
William of Clinton forced me to do it.

Barbara.   Forced you! You're President and will be forced?
The wounded lion, when overpowered,
will at least stamp his paw and wound the earth,
if nothing else, in his ferocious rage.
Will you, a lion and a king of beasts,
take your correction mildly, kiss the rod,
and fawn on Clinton with humility?
You have undone yourself, your sons, and me,
and have given the Clintons such power
that we'll live only by their sufferance.
To give the crown to these low-born yokels
is to assemble your own sepulcher
and creep into it far before your time.
His over-proud wife will sweep through the court,
contemptible harridan that she is.
She'll be eager to wreak vengeance on us,
consorting with witches and conjurers.
Albert of Tennessee, who hates our clan,
will help them in running the government,
filling its ranks with crud from Arkansas.
John of Arizona will bide his time.
And yet you will be safe? Such safety finds
the pale, trembling lamb surrounded by wolves.
Had I, a delicate woman, been there,
these peasants would have tossed me on their pikes
before I would have accepted such shame!
But you prefer your life to your honor.
And seeing you do, I divorce myself,
coward, from both your table and your bed,
until Congress overturns your action

by which my sons are disinherited.
Thus do I leave you, my spineless husband.
                [QUEEN STARTS TO LEAVE]
George I.   Coward!?   *[QUEEN HESITATES]*
You would let this mob kill the Prince.
I see no point in such a sacrifice.
I'm no coward. You're a loveless mother.

Barbara.   Those slain in valor fly straight to Heaven.
Even when the Prince was my only son,
I wanted my boy to achieve renown.
I would send him to the cruelest of wars
if he might return in martial triumph.
In seeing young George prove himself a man,
I'd feel no less joy than when he was born.
He must not live ignominiously;
he would – if he prefers exile to death.

George I.   You would have him die in this business?

Barbara.   If I had twelve sons and loved each the same,
I'd rather have eleven die nobly
than even one accused of cowardice.
                [EXIT QUEEN]
Clinton.   Enough. We must grant the commons their wish.
In plain view, George must surrender his crown,
so we can proceed without suspicion.
Willingly, he must make me his sole heir,
place into my hands his golden scepter,
and descend the throne, that I may ascend.

George I.   And so, I must shake off those regal thoughts
with which I reigned, though I have not yet learned
to insinuate, flatter, and bow down.
Give sorrow leave awhile to tutor me
to this submission. Yet I well recall
the support of these men. Were they not mine?

Did they not sometimes cry 'all hail!' to me?
And so did Judas cry to Jesus Christ.
But he, in twelve, found truth in all but one,
while I, in a nation, find it in none.
And what service must I now perform?

Clinton.   To do that office of your own good will
that tired majesty made you offer,
the resignation of your state and crown
to me as your heir and named successor.
Are you contented to resign the crown?

George I.   What should the President do now, submit?
Can I part with the name of President?
For God's sake, I must let the title go.
I'll give my jewels for a set of beads,
my gorgeous palace for a hermitage,
my gay apparel for an almsman's gown,
my figured goblets for a dish of wood,
my scepter for a pilgrim's walking staff,
my subjects for a set of carved relics,
and my large domain for a little grave.
I can see now that I must be nothing,
and pass the Presidency to Clinton.
Now mark me, how I will undo myself.
            [HANDS HIS CROWN TO CLINTON]
I give this heavy weight from off my head
            [GIVES HIS SCEPTER TO CLINTON]
and this unwieldy scepter from my hand,
the pride of royal sway from out my heart.
With my own tears I wash away my balm.
With my own hands I give away my crown,
with my own tongue deny my sacred state,
with my own breath release all duty's rites.
All pomp and majesty I do forswear.
My acts, decrees, and statutes I deny.
God pardon all oaths that are broke to me!

God keep all vows unbroke that swear to you!

Clinton.   In God's name, I'll ascend the regal throne.
And as this fratricidal struggle ends,
I'll use gently both friend and foe alike.
I am no Turk or infidel despot.
            [SPEAKS QUIETLY TO HIMSELF]
Now, I must consolidate my power
and not needlessly make new enemies.
In time, I'll make them all fall to their knees.
            [RAISES HIS VOICE AGAIN]
I would feel no joy seeing our fair earth
soiled with streams of dear blood it has fostered.
I thus spare the life of the President,
and those of his queen, sons, and counselors.
Yet I must banish them from our country,
except the ill old man, who is no threat;
him I'll keep near as proof of my mercy.
If his sons remained, their eagle-winged pride
and their hateful envy would wake our peace.
            [TURNS TO THE PRINCE]
The Prince, one-time heir, upon pain of life
shall not return to our fair dominions
but tread the stranger paths of banishment
until eight summers have enriched our fields.

Prince. *[LOOKS TO HIS FATHER, WHO NODS SADLY]*
Your will be done. This must my comfort be:
the sun that warms you here shall shine on me.

Clinton.   James, for you remains a heavier doom,
which I with some unwillingness pronounce.
There is no limit upon your exile;
the hopeless words of 'never to return'
I breathe against you, upon pain of life.

James.   A heavy sentence, and unexpected.
Then thus I turn me from my country's light,
to dwell in solemn shades of endless night.

Clinton.   Richard, you too shall suffer the same fate.

Richard.   I merit far better treatment than this –
reward for my service, not punishment.
Yet your will matches my master's wishes,
and I can see you will not change your mind.

Clinton.   Come, the three of you; take an oath with me.
Lay your banished hands on my new scepter,
and swear by the duty you owe to God
to keep the oath that I administer.
You never shall, so help you truth and God,
embrace each other's love in banishment;
nor never look upon each other's face.
You shall never meet to plot any ill
against me or my administration.

Prince.   I swear.

Richard.   As I do.

James.   And I swear as well.
          [LOOKS TO GEORGE I]
Farewell, my liege. Now no way can I stray,
save back to this land. All the world's my way.
          [MEMBERS OF THE MOB LET HIM GO; HE EXITS]
Clinton.   *[LOOKING AT DEPOSED PRESIDENT]*
You said, 'banish my sons to save their lives,'
and I have done so on your good advice.
Prince, farewell; and, elder George, bid him so:
eight years I banish him, and he shall go.

George I.   Come, come, my son, I'll send you on your way.
Had I your youth and cause, I would not stay.

Prince.   Then, America's ground, sweet soil, adieu;
my mother, and my nurse, that bears me yet!
Wherever I roam, boast of this I can,
though banished, yet a true American.

> *[ALL EXIT BUT RICHARD, WHO WALKS BEHIND
> THE OTHERS]*

Richard.   What a doleful pageant we just beheld.
Great woe is to come; children yet unborn
will feel this day as sharply as a thorn.
Yet what fate imposes, men must abide.
A man cannot resist both wind and tide.
So, sweet America, farewell for now.
God shield me from Clinton's angry frown,
that someday I can seize from him the crown.
His succession will be a fierce struggle.
His wife, that witch, is too old to bear sons;
and though she covets the crown for herself,
the nation will not accept her as chief.
Yet lewd Clinton cavorts with foul women,
so if diseases don't waste him away,
his loins may beget multiple claimants
to fight me for the golden time I want.
And, even worse, ahead of me in line
are the Prince, Jeb, John of Arizona,
and possibly Albert of Tennessee.
Why, then, do I dream of sovereignty?

I am too ambitious for my station.
If only my strength equaled my striving!
Well, say there is no power for Richard,
what other pleasure can the world afford?
I could deck my body in ornaments,
and charm sweet ladies with my words and looks,
seeking heaven in their inviting laps.
Oh miserable thought, more unlikely
to accomplish than twenty golden crowns!
Why, love forsook me in my mother's womb
by making me misshapen and deformed.

How can such a contorted man be loved?
Oh monstrous fault, to harbor such a thought!
Then, since this earth affords no joy to me,
but to command, check, and humiliate
people of breeding better than my own,
I'll make my heaven to dream on the throne.

  [EXIT]

Act IV. Scene I.—*Charleston, South Carolina. In a Field.*

[ENTER CHORUS]

Chorus.   Now with imagined wings, think of yourselves
flying past scenes spanning nearly eight years.
Suppose that, from your airborne vantage point,
you see Clinton form a government based
on high taxes and rancor for the rich.
Watch him surround himself with an odd mix
of Arkansas cronies, celebrities,
and – despite his populist rhetoric –
Wall Street money men and policy wonks.
Observe him as, obsessed with fund-raising,
he sells his time to the highest bidders,
sipping coffee or posing for pictures
with donors to his unending campaign.
See Clinton grow reckless playing Bacchus.
Behold him, trousers down, with an intern,
while his loathing wife fumes in the next room.
Hear howling conservatives in Congress
demand bloody revenge through impeachment.
Note that, though they have more corn than before,
the commons want different leadership,
as they tire of Clinton's misbehavior.
Watch the shamed man name Albert as his heir
and see Prince George return from banishment
to seek the restoration of his house.
Start to envision a coming struggle
between George and John of Arizona
for the chance to fight Albert for power.
          [EXIT]

Act IV. Scene II.—Charleston, South Carolina. In a Field.

[ENTER TOURNAMENT OFFICIALS, PRINCE
GEORGE, JOHN OF ARIZONA, AND A CROWD OF
ONLOOKERS]

Chairman. Marshal, demand of yonder champions
the cause of their arrival here in arms.
Ask them their names and orderly proceed
to swear them in the justice of their cause.

Marshal. In God's name, gentlemen, say who you are
and why you come thus clad in knightly arms,
against whom you come, what your quarrel is.
Speak truly, on your knighthood and your oath,
and so defend you heaven and your valor!
  [TRUMPETS SOUND]
John. My name, Sir, is John of Arizona.
I come here having made a sacred oath—
which God forbid a knight should violate—
to gain, through my devotion to justice,
the Presidency of this great country.
And, by the grace of God and this my arm,
I intend to vanquish all challengers.
As I truly fight, defend me heaven!
  [TRUMPETS SOUND]
Prince. George, son of the President by that name
am I, who ready here do stand in arms
to prove, by God's grace and my body's valor,
that I am the proper heir to the throne.
As I truly fight, defend me heaven!

Marshal. On pain of death, no person be so bold
or daring-hardy as to touch the lists.

Prince. Lord Marshall, John and I are like two men
who vow a long and weary pilgrimage.
Permit us a few words before we clash;
one of us will soon be still forever.

I'll begin by joining with all the world
in high praise of John of Arizona.
I do not think a braver gentleman,
more valiant, daring or bold, now lives
to grace this modern age with noble deeds.
Yet his claim to the throne is defective.
I am the first son of a President
and grandson to a noble Senator.
Though courageous, John is of common blood.
And though he is stern, he has feet of clay.
Not all great soldiers make great presidents.
He is visited nightly by furies,
who stoke a rage first kindled by torture.
He has fathered a child as black as pitch,
the fruit of fornication with a witch!
He lacks the temperament to govern well.
He can no longer share glory with me.
Two stars keep not their motion in one sphere;
nor can America have two leaders.

John. Nor shall it, young George; for the hour is come
to end the one of us; and don't you wish
your name in arms were now as great as mine!
I tell the world you remain a wanton!
Never was a prince such a libertine.
While I fought in jungles for my country,
and was captured by savage enemies,
you got drunk and high in idle comfort.
God will make me prosper in my just cause.

Prince. I can no longer bear your vanities.
[DRAWS HIS SWORD AND TURNS TO CROWD]
Friends, I place my fate in the hands of God.
So let no noble eye profane a tear
for me if I be gored with John's sharp spear.
As confident as a falcon in flight
against a bird do I with this man fight.

John. *[DRAWS HIS SWORD]*
My soul celebrates this feast of battle,
just as a freed captive, dancing with joy,
craves the chance to make his way in the world.
I put my case before God as my judge.
                    [THEY FIGHT; JOHN IS WOUNDED AND FALLS]
John. Oh, Prince George, you have robbed me of my youth!
I can better bear the loss of my life
than the loss of my proud titles to you.
I would say more, but the cold hand of death
lies on my tongue: no, John, you are now dust
and food for—
                    [LOSES CONSCIOUSNESS]
Prince. —for worms, brave man of great heart.
Ill-weaved ambition, how much are you shrunk!
When this body did contain a spirit,
a nation for it was too small a bound;
but now two paces of the vilest earth
is room enough. This earth that bears you dead
bears not alive so stout a gentleman.

Marshal. *[KNEELING OVER JOHN]*
My Lord, he is still breathing and alive.

Prince. Tend to him. I leave in search of Albert.
                    [PRINCE EXITS]

Act IV. Scene III.—Washington. The Capitol.

[ENTER JAMES OF HOUSTON AND RICHARD OF WYOMING]

James. How now, my Lord Richard of Wyoming?

Richard. How is the Prince?

James. He's exceedingly well.
To gain the throne, he must win Florida;
but his brother is the Governor there,
and controls all the levers of power.
So our campaign is quite optimistic.

Richard. I fear the service I did his father
has left me open to all injuries.

James. Indeed I think the young Prince loves you not.

Richard. I know he does not, and do arm myself
to be ready for what time may bring me.
But James, what I did, I did in honor,
led by the impartial sense of my soul.

James. Here comes the Prince and future President.
        [ENTER PRINCE GEORGE]
Richard. Good morrow, and God save your majesty!

Prince. That title 'majesty' is right indeed.
We just received word from my brother Jeb
that Albert has been soundly defeated.
We've set a date for my coronation.
        [JAMES AND RICHARD FALL TO THEIR KNEES]
Yet this new, gorgeous garment, majesty,
sits not so easy on me as you think.
My lords, I sense fear in your demeanor.
I'm no barbarous Turkish potentate,
but plan to be an enlightened ruler.

[LOOKS AT RICHARD]
You are, I think, assured, I love you not.

Richard.   I am assured, if I be judged rightly,
your majesty has no cause to hate me.

Prince.   No!? How might a prince of my hopes forget
the great indignities you laid on me?
You rebuked me and harshly punished me –
the likely heir to the Presidency!

Richard.   I acted as agent of your father.
The image of his power lay in me.
While I administered his royal law,
your highness, then a lad, insulted me
and showed disrespect for the rule of law,
the very form of your father's justice.
You being an offender to your father,
I gave bold way to my authority,
and did punish you. If the deed were ill,
then be contented, when you wear the crown,
to have your son set your decrees aside,
to trip the course of law, and blunt the sword
that protects the safety of your person.
After considering this, sentence me.

Prince.   You are right, Richard; and you weigh this well.
Therefore take on the Vice Presidency.
I intend to see your honors increase
until you live to see a son of mine
offend you and obey you, as I did.
As you committed me to royal law,
I do now commit into your wise hands
the unstained sword that you used to carry.
You shall be as a father to my youth.
My voice will speak words you put in my ear,
and I will formulate my policies

based on your experience and wisdom.
I want to build on my father's glories,
to mock the expectation of the world,
to frustrate prophecies of disaster,
and to overcome rotten opinion,
which takes me for what I have seemed to be.
Soon I must recruit a new Cabinet.
I must find advisers who can make me
ready for war or peace, or both at once.
In this, Richard, you wield the foremost hand.

Richard.   One celebrated name comes straight to mind:
my old mentor Donald of Illinois.
He'd be a perfect Minister of War.

Prince.   Then he'll be in charge of our foreign wars.
But first, I feel a fervor for tax cuts.
          [EXIT ALL]

Act IV. Scene IV.—*The Streets of Washington.*

[ENTER SIR JOHN PIKESTAFF AND MERCHANT]

Jack.   Young George's coronation is over.
The President's train will be passing through.
As you know, this lad has been my best friend,
my source of funds, and my finest pupil.
I've taught him what he knows of government.
I can lobby him for favors for you;
he'll steer contracts to your corporation.
I will wink at him as he walks by us.
Watch for the friendly look he will give me.

Merchant.   You better be right. Or you still owe me.
I won't waive your debts without those contracts.
> *[SHOUTS AND TRUMPETS SOUND; ENTER*
> *PRESIDENT GEORGE II (FORMERLY THE*
> *PRINCE), VICE PRESIDENT RICHARD, DONALD*
> *OF ILLINOIS, AND OTHERS]*

Jack.   God save you, President George, my sweet boy!

George II.   Lord Vice President, speak to that vain man.

Richard.   Have you lost your wits? You can't talk like that.

Jack.   My President! I speak to you, my Jove!

George II.   I don't know you, old man; fall to prayers.
How white hairs do ill become a jester.
I have long dreamed of such a kind of man,
so pot-bellied, so old, and so profane;
but, being awake, I despise my dream.
Don't reply to me with a foolish jest.
Don't presume that I am the thing I was;
for God knows, and so shall the world perceive,
that I have turned away my former self.
So will I those who kept me company.
I therefore banish you, on pain of death,

not to come within ten miles of me.
For your sustenance, I will allow you
enough to keep you from doing evil.
Richard, please take care of these tasks. Move on.
>   *[EXIT PRESIDENT GEORGE II AND HIS TRAIN]*
Merchant.   Sir John, I must ask you to pay your debts.
I want to take the money home with me.

Jack.   I'm afraid that can hardly be, dear friend.
Do not grieve over this seeming setback.
I shall be sent for in private to him.
Look you, he must seem this way to the world.
You should not feel fear for your advancements.
I'll be the man yet who shall make you great.

Merchant.   I cannot perceive how, unless you give
me your doublet and stuff me out with straw.
I beseech you for half of what you owe.

Jack.   In time, I will be as good as my word;
but what you heard just now was a pretense.
The President will send for me tonight.
>   *[RE-ENTER THE VICE PRESIDENT, DONALD, AND*
>   *OFFICERS]*
Richard.   Go, carry Sir John Pikestaff off to jail.
>   *[EXIT PIKESTAFF AND OFFICERS]*
Donald.   Did you know that Congress is in session?

Richard.   The President has a new agenda.

Donald.   I will lay odds that, before this year ends,
we bear our civil swords and native fire
into Babylon in a Holy War.
I heard a bird sing of an invasion,
and it seemed to please the new President.

Richard.   That would please you too?

Donald.   Absolutely so.

Richard.   Restoration of conservative rule
ends the long winter of our discontent.
A glorious new summer is at hand;
the dark clouds of Clintonism are gone.
Now are our brows bound with victory wreaths,
our battered arms hung up for monuments.
Grim-visaged war has smoothed his wrinkled front
and now, instead of mounting armored steeds
to frighten the souls of adversaries,
he skips nimbly in a lady's chamber
to the lascivious sounds of a lute.
But I scorn and hate effeminate peace.
I don't delight in passing time in ease.
I do not strut before wanton women
or admire my image in the mirror.
Nature cheated me of fair proportion;
I am not a handsome man, but grotesque.
I was born before my time and backward,
a deformed lump; and I walk so lamely
that dogs bark at me as I pass by them.
Therefore, since I cannot prove a lover
to while away these fair well-spoken days,
I am determined to prove a villain
and hate the idle pleasures of these days.
I will lay plots to set great nations in
deadly hate the one against the other.
If the President is as true and just
as I am subtle, false and treacherous,
then America will soon be at war.
My shiny pate may never wear the crown,
but through the ignorant youth I can rule.
He knows more of taverns than of the world.
I'll bear the heavy weight of government,
while he enjoys the honor and his ease.

[EXIT RICHARD]

Act IV. Scene V.—Washington. An ante-chamber in the President's Palace.

[ENTER RICHARD AND BISHOP GERALD]

Richard. There is a bill on the President's desk
of great importance to your supporters.
Congress passed it when Clinton held the throne,
but in that stormy and unquiet time
he failed to act on the legislation.
It would eliminate tax exemptions
enjoyed by churches throughout the country.

Gerald. But how, my lord, shall we resist it now?

Richard. Let's think about it. If George signs the bill,
religious leaders would lose half their wealth.
Their empires of faith would crumble to dust.

Gerald. This would drink deep.

Richard. This would drain the whole cup.

Gerald. What can we do to ensure a veto?

Richard. The President is full of fair regard.

Gerald. And a true lover of the holy Church.

Richard. There was no promise of this in his youth.
His rise to the nation's highest office
has brought on a transformation in him.
When he lifted his hand from the Bible
after swearing the oath of his office,
his former wildness, mortified in him,
seemed to perish at that very moment.
Never was such a sudden scholar made.
Never came reformation in a flood

with such a strong current, scouring faults.

Gerald.   America is blessed by this man's change.
But what about that bill passed by Congress?
Is his Majesty inclined to sign it?

Richard.   Although at first he seemed indifferent,
I think he's now leaning towards a veto.
I suggested to him that your churches
might give him their support on another
matter of greatest importance to him.
To undertake war against Babylon,
he needs greater sums than the clergy have
given any of his predecessors.

Gerald.   How did he react to this suggestion?

Richard.   With good acceptance by his Majesty,
though I had far too little time with him
to complete our discourse on the subject.
We were interrupted by messengers
who informed us that Babylonian
ambassadors sought discussion with him.

Gerald.   Has he yet received these foreign agents?

Richard.   No. The audience is at four o'clock.

Gerald.   That hour is drawing very near at hand.

Richard.   Then let us go talk with the President
before the Ambassadors are brought in.

Gerald.   I'll wait upon you, and speak as needed.
            [EXIT]

Act IV. Scene VI. – *Washington. The Oval Chamber in the Palace*
> *[ENTER PRESIDENT GEORGE II; VICE*
> *PRESIDENT RICHARD; CONDOLEEZZA,*
> *COUNTESS OF STANFORD; BISHOP GERALD;*
> *COLIN OF NEW YORK; AND ATTENDANTS]*

George II. Where is my gracious Minister of War?

Richard. Not here in presence.

George II. Send for him, Richard.
> *[EXIT RICHARD]*

Condi. Shall we call in the ambassadors, liege?

George II. Not yet dear lady; I should be resolved,
before I hear them, of some things of weight
that task my thoughts concerning Babylon.
> *[ENTER RICHARD AND MINISTER OF WAR*
> *DONALD]*

Donald. God and his angels guard your sacred throne,
and make you long become it!

George II. I thank you.
My learned lord, I pray you to proceed,
and justly and piously explain how
domestic and international law
instruct us on the great question of war.
And God forbid, my dear and faithful lord,
that you interpret sacred principles
to expound claims not in accord with truth;
for God does know how many now in health
shall drop their blood as a consequence of
actions that your words shall incite me to.
And therefore take heed how you provoke me,
how you awake my sleeping sword of war.
I charge you, in the name of God, take heed;
for never did two such dominions contend
without great losses of patriot blood.
If you are wrong in advocating war,

each drop of innocent blood spent in vain
will be a woe and complaint against you.
Under this conjuration, speak, my lord.

Donald.   Then hear me, gracious sovereign, and you peers,
who owe yourselves, your lives, and services,
to this imperial throne. War is just
and lawful under current conditions.
International law sets up no bar
but this, which our enemies throw at us:
that only defensive war can be just.
They say war here would not be in 'defense.'
Yet their own authors faithfully affirm
that America has spurned that precept,
routinely launching wars of aggression.
This one international norm applies
to all nations but the United States,
with its exceptional role in the world.
Heathen native tribes once controlled these shores,
which Christians wrested from them by brute force.
And our ancestors seized California
from Mexico for its bounteous soils.
Now that crops bloom there, shall we give it back?
Then does it well appear that this precept
was never intended for our land.
But even if international law
did apply to God-blessed America,
a war against Saddam would still be right.
He stockpiles weapons of mass destruction,
and supported the evil terrorists
who launched strikes on New York and Washington.
And yet Saddam himself taunts and mocks us
by invoking international law.

George II. May I with right and conscience launch this war?

Donald. The sin upon my head, dread sovereign!
Stand for your own, unwind your bloody flag.

Look back to your gallant predecessors;
draw inspiration from their examples.
Think of fearless Andrew of Tennessee,
that lion who foraged in English blood.
He played a tragedy at New Orleans,
defeating the full power of Britain.

Richard. Awake remembrance of these valiant dead,
and with your mighty arm renew their feats.
You are their heir; you sit upon their throne.
You are in the very morning of youth,
ripe for exploits and great enterprises.

Condi. Your brother rulers from other nations
do all expect that you should rouse yourself,
as did the former lions of your blood.

Donald. They know your Grace has cause and means and might.
No earlier wartime President had
richer nobles or more loyal subjects.

Gerald. Oh, let brave men follow you in battle
with blood and sword and fire to do the right!
In aid, we of the spiritual class
will raise your Highness such a mighty sum
as never did the clergy at one time
bring in to any of your ancestors.

George II. Call the ambassadors from Babylon.
                   [EXIT SOME ATTENDANTS]
Now I am well resolved; and, by God's help
and yours, the noble sinews of our strength,
our military will shock and awe foul
Babylon or break it all to pieces.
                   [ENTER AMBASSADORS]
Now we're well prepared to learn the pleasure
of Saddam's son Uday; for I hear that
your greeting is from him, not his father.

Ambassador.   May it please your Majesty to give us
leave to be frank in stating our message?

George II.   I'm no tyrant, but a Christian ruler,
in whose mind reason keeps passion in check,
as wretches are fettered in our prisons.
Therefore with frank and with uncurbed plainness
tell us Lord Uday's mind.

Ambassador.   Thus then, in short:
your Highness recently sent Lord Saddam
a demand that he disgorge arms stockpiles
you claim threaten the shores of your nation.
In answer to this, the Prince our master
says that your brashness is proof of your youth.
He advises you that control of our
country cannot be won through merriment.
You cannot revel into power there.
He therefore sends you this box of treasure,
and insists that he hear no more of you.
            [HANDS BOX TO VICE PRESIDENT]
George II.   What treasure, Richard?

Richard.   Tennis balls, my liege.

George II.   I am glad Uday is so droll with me.
His present and your pains I thank you for.
When we have matched our rackets to these balls,
we will, by God's grace, play a set that shall
strike his father's crown into the hot sand.
Tell Uday he's made a match with a foe
whose returning strokes will overwhelm him.
Oh, I understand him well, how he baits
me by ridiculing my wilder days,
not measuring what use I made of them.
Tell Lord Uday that I will keep my state,
be a conqueror, and show my greatness,

when I do rouse myself in fury and
seize for myself the throne of Babylon.
Although I set aside my majesty
while still but a Prince or in banishment,
I will rise now with so full a glory
that I'll dazzle the eyes of all the world,
and strike young Uday blind to look on me.
So tell the jesting Prince this mock of his
has turned his tennis balls to cannon balls.
And his soul, not mine, shall stand charged for the
wasteful vengeance that shall be caused by them.
Thousands of widows will grieve for husbands;
thousands of mothers will grieve for their sons;
and thousands of your people yet unborn
will have cause to curse Uday's foolish jest.
But this lies all within the will of God,
to whom I do appeal, and in whose name,
tell your Lord Uday, I am coming on,
to seek revenge and fight a noble cause.
So get you hence in peace; and tell Lord Uday
his jest will savor but of shallow wit,
when thousands more weep than did laugh at it.
Convey them with safe conduct. Fare you well.

[EXIT AMBASSADORS]

Richard.   This was a merry message, your Highness.

George II.   We hope to make the sender blush at it.
Therefore, my lords, omit no happy hour
that may be used to further our purpose;
for now I have no thought in me but war.
We'll chide this Uday at his father's door.
Go raise the funds we will need to invade.
Undertake all preparation that may
with swiftness add more feathers to our wings.
Thus, let every man now task his thought
so that this Holy War may soon be fought.   *[EXIT ALL]*

Act IV. Scene VII.—Washington. The Palace.

Chorus.   Now America's young men are on fire,
and put aside all frivolous pursuits.
Now armorers thrive. The thought of honor
reigns alone in each patriotic breast.
For now expectation sits in the air,
and makes soldiers dream of coming booty
promised to the President's followers.
The foe, advised by good intelligence
of all this most dreadful preparation,
shake in their fear, and with diplomacy
seek to thwart the President's purposes.
Oh America, with your mighty heart,
how strong you would be if all walked in step!
But some oppose the preemptive conflict;
Barack the Moor calls the war unprovoked.
For now, though, few share the dark rebel's qualms.
>   *[EXIT CHORUS; ENTER VICE PRESIDENT AND*
>   *MINISTER OF WAR]*

Richard.   By God, we must watch this Barack with care.
How smooth and even he does bear himself,
as if allegiance sat in his bosom.
Yet the traitor speaks out against our war.

Donald.   The President must learn what he intends.
Afraid to take arms, the coward would doom
his sovereign's life to death and treachery!
>   *[TRUMPET SOUNDS. ENTER THE PRESIDENT,*
>   *COLIN, CONDI, AND ATTENDANTS]*

George II.   Now the winds are fair, and we can leave port.
My Lord Richard, and my kind Lord Donald,
and you, gentle Condi, give me your thoughts.
Do you think the troops we take with us will
cut a passage through Saddam's defenses?

Donald.   No doubt, my liege, if each man does his best.

George II. I don't doubt that, since all are persuaded
of the justice of our most noble cause.
We carry with us not a single heart
not in complete harmony with our own
and leave behind not one who does not wish
us success in our role of conqueror.

Richard. Never was ruler better feared and loved
than is your Majesty. Yet one subject
will not serve you with a heart filled with zeal.
Barack of Chicago, known as the Moor,
rails against your just war on Babylon.
You must punish him, or your lenience
will inspire more examples of his kind.

Condi. You'd show him mercy if you spare his life
after making him taste much correction.

George II. Call in the Moor.
       [ENTER BARACK OF CHICAGO]
Barack. Greetings, my noble liege.

George II. What shall I say to you, youthful Barack,
you ungrateful and inhuman creature?
By opposing my holiest of wars
you give our enemies aid and comfort.

Barack. I have only done what I thought was right.
Though I confess no fault, I appeal for
mercy at your Highness's mighty hands.

George II. God spare you in his mercy! I have none.
Those who are not with me are against me.
Traitor, you've conspired against my person
and joined with my most despised enemy.
You would have delivered me to slaughter,
my nobles and my peers to servitude,

my subjects to oppression and contempt,
and this whole nation into desolation.
If we left homeland defense to your ilk,
invading armies would enjoy our lands,
lie with our wives, and ravish our daughters.
If punishment did not create martyrs,
I would make sure you died a painful death.
But I will not make that foolish mistake,
though you seek the ruin of your country
and its people; therefore leave my presence.
God give you patience to endure your shame,
and light to guide you to true repentance.

Barack.   My most potent, grave, and reverend liege,
I shall do my best to serve my country
in a way that also serves my conscience.
        [EXIT BARACK]
George II.   Now, lords, let us undertake our crusade.
Our enterprise will bring all of us fame.
Dear countrymen, let us put out to sea,
and thus place our fates in the hands of God.
I am President of America,
and will yet preside over Babylon!
        [EXIT ALL BUT COLIN OF NEW YORK]
Colin.   My oath of office requires me to ask
what rub or what impediment there is
to thwart the mangling of poor, naked Peace.
Richard and Donald, who in youth pursued
scholarship rather than arms, jump to war.
I fought in their place, and bear their wounds too.
Oh graceless men, they know not what they do.
Yet young George is my Commander in Chief.
His father, my elder, no longer reigns.
And as a soldier, I must be loyal.
I therefore must suppress my misgivings.
        [ENTER BARACK, OUT OF HEARING OF COLIN]
If my divining thoughts prove to be true,

this pretty lad will prove our country's bliss.
His looks are full of peaceful majesty,
his head by nature framed to wear a crown,
his hand to wield a scepter, and himself
likely in time to bless a regal throne.

[EXIT COLIN; A MOMENT LATER, EXIT BARACK]

Act V. Scene I.—Baghdad.   Saddam's Palace.

*[FLOURISH; ENTER SADDAM, UDAY, TARIQ, AND
ATTENDANTS]*

Saddam.   America comes at us with full strength;
so we must build our defenses with care.

Uday.   My most wise and illustrious father,
it is proper to arm against the foe;
for peace should not so soften a nation
as to make it open to invasion.
Even where no war or quarrel exists,
strong fortifications should be maintained.
But let us do it with no show of fear –
as though we had heard that America
busies itself with holiday dancing;
for she has such an idle President,
my good liege, that no nation should fear her.

Tariq.   Prince Uday, you are much mistaken in
your estimation of this President.
Your ambassadors say that he heard them
with great state, and yet spoke with modesty;
that he is well supplied with counselors;
and that he is terrible in his wrath.

Saddam.   I think that young President George is strong.
        [ENTER A MESSENGER]
Messenger.   Ambassadors sent by President George
do crave admittance to your Majesty.

Saddam.   We'll give them audience. Go and bring them.
        [EXIT MESSENGER]
You see this chase is hotly followed, friends.
        *[RE-ENTER MESSENGER WITH DONALD AND
        TRAIN]*
Saddam.   You're here on behalf of the President?

Donald.   I am, and he greets your Majesty thus.
He warns, in the name of God Almighty,
that you must divest yourself, and lay down,
the borrowed glories that by gift of God,
by the laws of nature and of nations,
belong to him and to his heirs – namely,
the crown of Babylon and the honors
that pertain thereto by custom of time.
He bids you then resign your golden crown,
wrongly kept from him, the true challenger.

Saddam.   Or else what consequences will follow?

Donald.   Bloody constraint; for if you hide the crown,
even in your hearts, he will rake for it.
Therefore in fierce tempest he is coming,
in thunder and in earthquake, like a Jove,
so that if asking fails, he will compel.
And he bids you, in the Lord's holy name,
to deliver the crown and take mercy
on the wretched souls this hungry war will
swallow in its vast jaws. If you refuse,
then on your head, not his, will lie the blame
for blood that shall flow. This is his message –
unless Prince Uday be in presence here,
to whom expressly I bring greeting too.

Uday.   I am Prince Uday. What is his greeting?

Donald.   Scorn and defiance, slight regard, contempt.
And he says that if your father Saddam
does not freely grant all of his demands
and beg pardon for your rude tennis balls,
my liege will come for you with such a zeal
that underground caverns shall close to you,
from fear of his Majesty's hot fury.

Uday.   Tell him that, if my father seeks a truce,

it is against my will; for I desire
nothing more than to fight this President,
known for his youth and vanity, not arms.
To that end, I mocked him with tennis balls.

Donald.   He'll make this lavish palace shake for it.

Saddam.   Tomorrow you shall learn our mind in full.

Donald.   Send us your news with all speed, so that the
President does not arrive here himself
to know the reason for your long delay;
for his troops are in this land already.

Saddam.   You shall soon be informed of our response.
A night is but small breath and little pause
to answer matters of this consequence.
            [EXIT ALL]

Act V. Scene II.—Outskirts of Baghdad.

[ENTER MESSENGER, PRESIDENT, AND COLIN OF NEW YORK]

Messenger.   You know my office by my uniform.

George II.   Well then, I know you; what shall I know of you?

Messenger.   My master's mind.

George II.   Unfold it.

Messenger.   He says thus.
Although he will not surrender his crown,
he offers instead his daughter Rana,
and with her a dowry of huge estates.

George II.   Surely he already knows my answer.
If he truly wants peace, he must buy it
with full agreement to all our demands.
You do your office fairly. Now turn back
and tell Saddam I do not seek him now.
Yet, God willing, tell him we will come on.
If we may pass into Baghdad, we will;
but if we be hindered, we'll discolor
your brown soil with the red blood of your troops.
The sum of all our answer is but this:
we would not seek a battle as we are;
but neither, as we are, will we shun it.

Messenger.   I shall tell him so. Thanks to your Highness.
          [EXIT MESSENGER]
Colin.   I hope they will not come upon us now.

George II.   We are in God's hands, Colin, not in theirs.
We have no need of overwhelming force,
as your rival Donald keeps telling us.
Though we have five men to twenty of theirs,

I doubt not, Colin, of our victory.

[EXIT]

Act V. Scene III.—Baghdad. Saddam's Palace.

*[ENTER SADDAM, UDAY, TARIQ, AND
ATTENDANTS]*

Saddam. Will it never be morning?

Tariq. It will soon.
[ENTER MESSENGER]
Messenger. My lord Saddam, the President will not
marry your daughter, but prefers to fight.
He is fifteen hundred paces from here.

Uday. If the Americans had any sense,
they would run away. Oh, but that they lack.
Our splendid appearance and sheer numbers
will suck the courage right out of their souls.
There won't be work enough for all our hands.
We will see, as we come onto the field,
Americans crouch down in fear and yield.

Saddam. Now is it time to arm. Come, shall we start?
[EXIT]

Act V.   Scene IV.—*The American camp outside Baghdad.*

>*[ENTER PRESIDENT, RICHARD, DONALD, AND COLIN]*

George II.   Lend me your cloak, Sir Richard.   Gentlemen,
convey my good wishes to your colleagues;
and shortly invite them all to my tent.

Richard.   We shall, my liege.

Colin.   Shall I attend your Grace?

George II.   No, good knight; go with Richard and Donald.
I and my bosom must debate awhile,
and I would have no other company.
>*[EXIT ALL BUT THE PRESIDENT; ENTER SERGEANT; PRESIDENT PULLS CLOAK OVER HEAD]*

Is not that the morning that breaks yonder?

Sergeant.   I think it is; but we have no great cause
to desire the approach of day and light.
We can see the beginning of the day;
I fear we'll never see the end of it.
Who are you?

George II.   A friend.

Sergeant.   Who is your captain?

George II.   That most gallant knight Sir Thomas of Franks.

Sergeant.   A good commander and kind gentleman.
Tell me, how does he perceive our chances?

George II.   Like those of men wrecked on a sandy shore,
who look to be washed off by the next tide.

Sergeant.   Has he shared these thoughts with the President?

George II.   No; nor would it be proper to do so.
The President is but a man like me.
Flowers smell to him as they do to me.
The sky looks to him as it does to me.
Take away his pomp and ceremony,
in his nakedness he is but a man.
And though his desires mount higher than ours,
yet when they stoop, they stoop as low as ours.
Thus when he learns there are reasons for fear,
he will suffer doubt, just as we feel it.
And his face will show the dread in his soul,
disheartening and weakening his troops.
That's why Presidents must not hear bad news.

Sergeant.   He may show what outward courage he will;
but I believe, as hot as it is here,
he would rather be in flames to his neck
than to be stuck here in this sandy hell.

George II.   I will give you my honest opinion:
he'd rather be here than anywhere else.

Sergeant.   Then I wish that he were here by himself:
being rich, he would surely be ransomed,
and many poor soldiers' lives would be saved.

George II.   I can't believe that you love him so ill
as to wish that he fight here all alone.
I heard him say he would not be ransomed.
I could not die anywhere so content
as in the President's brave company,
his cause being just and honorable.

Sergeant.   That's more than we know, or should seek to learn.
We know enough if we know that we are
the President's subjects, who must heed him.

If his cause be wrong, our obedience
to him wipes the crime of it out of us.
But if his cause is not just and righteous,
the President himself has a heavy
reckoning to make on great Judgment Day.

Even if the President's war is just,
if some of his soldiers do not die well
and thus are damned on the Day of Judgment,
it will be a black mark against his soul.
I think few die well who die in battle;
for who can act with Christian charity
when in a rage to kill an enemy?

George II. You are wrong, friend; the President does not
answer for the endings his soldiers meet.
God alone chooses who lives and who dies.
Some perish for sins committed before,
others for crimes inflicted during war.
No matter how spotless his cause may be,
no President seeking divine justice
through war goes with all unspotted soldiers.
Every subject owes duty to his lord;
but each subject's soul is his very own.
Therefore every soldier in the wars should
do as every sick man in his bed does:
wash every speck of sin from his conscience.
Dying so, death is to him a blessing.

Sergeant. It is certain that when a man dies ill,
the blame is on his own head and none else.
I'll fight lustily for the President
but for now I must finish my patrol.
   [EXIT SERGEANT]
George II. Upon the President! Let's lay on him
our lives, our souls, our debts, our fearful wives,
our children, and our sins. He must bear all.
This is the hard condition of greatness.

What infinite heart's ease must Presidents
neglect that private citizens enjoy!
And what do we have that they can't enjoy
but ceremony – dull ceremony?
And what are you, you idol Ceremony?
What do you drink but poisoned flattery?
Oh, you proud dream that plays so subtly with
a President's repose and peace of mind.
I know what little solace you offer
when my worldly cares deprive me of sleep.
What good are the balm, the scepter, the ball,
the sword, the mace, the crown imperial,
the throne I sit on, and the tide of pomp
that beats upon the high shore of this world?
They can't help me, in my majestic bed,
sleep half so soundly as the wretched slave.
And but for ceremony, such a wretch,
winding up days with toil and nights with sleep,
would have more comforts than a president.

        [ENTER COLIN]

Colin. My lord, your nobles, finding you absent,
are searching through our camp looking for you.

George II. Good old knight, collect them all at my tent.
I'll be there soon.

Colin. I shall do it, my lord.   *[EXIT]*

George II. *[KNEELING]*
Oh God of battles, steel my soldiers' hearts;
possess them not with fear. Take from them now
the sense of reckoning, so that our foe's
large numbers will not pluck their hearts from them.
Today, oh Lord, do not think of the sins
I wrought in restoring our dynasty.
I slandered good John of Arizona,
accusing that noble soul of gross vice.
I pledged a humble foreign policy,

but quietly planned to build an empire.
For these sins, I have wept more contrite tears
than drops of blood have issued from John's wounds.
More will I do, though all is worth nothing,
since my penitence comes after my sins,
imploring forgiveness for bad actions.

      [ENTER CONDI]

Condi. My liege!

George II. My dear lady Condoleezza,
I know your errand, and will go with you.

      [EXIT]

Act V. Scene V.—The American Camp Outside of Baghdad.

[ENTER RICHARD, DONALD, AND COLIN]

Richard.   Where is our commander, the President?

Donald.   He rode to view our foe's assembled troops.

Colin.   Of fighting men, they have three-score thousand.
That's five to one against us; and they're fresh.
God's arm strike with us! These are fearful odds.

Donald.   Lord Colin, you are too pessimistic.
Your preference for overwhelming force,
instead of smaller and more nimble armies,
would force us to fight like an elephant.
With fewer men, we are fast and agile.
        [ENTER THE PRESIDENT]
Colin.   Oh that we had here but one ten thousandth
of the men in America today!

George II.   Who's he that wishes so, my lord Colin?
If we are doomed to die, we are enough
to do our country loss; and if to live,
the fewer men, the greater the honor.
God's will! I pray you, wish not one man more.
By Jove, I am not covetous for gold.
Nor do I care who feeds at my expense.
But if it's a sin to covet honor,
I am the most offending soul alive.
No, wish not a man from America.
God's peace! I don't want to share our honor
with one more man arrived from our country.
And any here with no stomach to fight,
let him depart; his passport shall be made,
and crowns for convoy put into his purse.
We would not die in that man's company
who fears his fellowship to die with us.

Today will come the Battle of Baghdad,
as the bards and chroniclers will call it.
He who outlives this day, and comes home safe,
will stand on tip-toes when this day is named,
and rouse himself upon hearing of it.
He who shall live this day, and see old age,
will strip his sleeve and show neighbors his scars,
and say 'These wounds I received in Baghdad.'
This fair date in April shall never pass
from this day to the ending of the world,
but we in it shall all be remembered;
for he today who sheds his blood with me
shall be my brother. Be he a vile serf,
this day shall ennoble his condition.
And men now in bed in America
shall think themselves accursed they were not here,
and hold their manhood cheap while any speaks
who fought with us today.
          [ENTER CONDI]
Condi.   My sovereign lord,
Prepare yourself and your forces with speed:
Our enemy is ready for battle.

George II.   All things are ready, if our minds be so.

Colin.   Perish the man whose mind is backward now!

George II.   You don't wish more help from America?

Colin.   God's will, my liege! Were you and I alone,
without more help, we could fight this battle!

George II.   Why, now you've wished away five thousand men,
which I would prefer to having one more.
You know your places. God be with you all!

Donald.   My lord, most humbly on my knee I beg
the honor to lead our vanguard forward.

George II. Take it, brave friend; for you've earned the honor.
Now we must throw ourselves into the breach
and either win or leave heaps of our dead.
In peace, nothing so well becomes a man
as modest stillness and humility.
But when the blast of war blows in our ears,
imitate the action of the tiger!
Stiffen the sinews, summon up the blood,
disguise fair nature with hard-favored rage;
then lend the eye a terrible aspect.
Now set the teeth and stretch the nostril wide;
hold hard the breath, and muster energy
to its full height. Onward Americans,
whose blood comes from fathers proved in battle.
Do not dishonor your mothers; and prove
that those you call fathers did beget you.
Nobles, be good examples to soldiers
of lesser blood; and teach them how to war.
And you, good yeomen, whose limbs were made in
America, show us here your mettle.
Let's swear that you are nobles for today;
for there is none of you so mean and base
who has not noble luster in his eyes.
I see you stand like greyhounds in the slips,
straining upon the start. The game's afoot:
follow your spirit; and upon this charge
cry 'God for George and the United States!'
Soldiers in our noble cause, march away;
and how you please, oh God, dispose the day!
       [EXIT; BATTLE BREAKS OUT]

Act V.   Scene VI.—On the Battlefield of Baghdad.

[ENTER SADDAM, UDAY, TARIQ, AND OTHERS]

Tariq.   All is confounded!   All our ranks are broke.
Reproach and everlasting shame mock us.
Oh malicious fortune!
           [SOUNDS OF BATTLE]
Don't run away!   *[SOLDIERS FLEE]*
Oh the lasting shame! Let us stab ourselves.
[TURNING TO UDAY] This is the President you called idle!

Uday.   We can retreat without surrendering;
we can become guerrilla insurgents.
I'm heir to the Babylonian throne.
I'll leave for now; later I'll come back home.

Saddam.   We can fight these dastards another day.
           [EXIT ALL]

Act V. Scene VII—On the Battlefield of Baghdad.

> *[ENTER PRESIDENT, VICE PRESIDENT, DONALD,
> COLIN, AND CONDI]*

Richard. Here comes the herald of Saddam, my liege.
> *[ENTER MESSENGER]*
Donald. His eyes are humbler than they used to be.

George II. How now! Why have you come here, messenger?
Do you intend to take me for ransom?
Don't you know I'll never yield for ransom?

Messenger. No, I come for charitable license,
that we may wander on this bloody field
to list our dead, and then to bury them,
to sort our nobles from our common men.
Let us view the field safely, and dispose
of our dead bodies.

George II. I tell you truly,
I don't know if the day be ours or yours;
for yet many of your horsemen appear
and move about the field.

Messenger. The day is yours.

George II. Praise be to God, and not our strength, for it!
I grant your request. I am no tyrant.
> *[EXIT MESSENGER]*
Major combat operations thus end.
My friends, we have accomplished our mission!
> *[EXIT ALL BUT COLIN]*
Colin. This victory may be illusory.
Our foes melted away too readily,
perhaps to regroup as a rebellion.
I fear we lack a sufficient army
to quash a guerrilla insurgency
or to win hearts with our humanity. *[EXIT]*

Act V. Scene VIII—Tikrit.

[ENTER SADDAM, UDAY, TARIQ, AND OTHERS]

Saddam.   The Americans have taken Baghdad,
but the countryside still belongs to us.

Tariq.   My lord, if we do not renew the fight,
we would abandon our beloved country,
and yield this land to a barbarous horde.

Uday.   Our madams mock at us and plainly say
our mettle is bred out, and they will give
their bodies to the lust of invaders
and spawn a race of bastard warriors.

Saddam.   Where is our messenger? Someone find him.
Let him greet George with our sharp defiance.
Up, Muslims, and, with spirit of honor
sharper than your swords, launch a rebellion.

Tariq.   This bold spirit reveals your greatness, liege.

Saddam.   Now go forth, Lord Tariq and Muslims all,
and quickly bring us word of George's fall.
        [EXIT ALL]

Act V. Scene IX—American Headquarters in Baghdad.

[ENTER PRESIDENT, VICE PRESIDENT, DONALD,
COLIN, AND CONDI, FOLLOWED BY
MESSENGER]

George II. Welcome, noble fellow. What's your errand?

Messenger. My master Saddam gives you this message.
'Though my army seemed dead, it did but sleep.
I could have defeated you in Baghdad,
but decided not to burst your pimple
until it was ripe for full explosion.
Now I speak at an opportune moment,
and my voice is proud and imperial.
President George, repent of your folly,
see your weakness, and admire my patience.
I will drive you out of this holy land.
Yet as your countrymen make strong weapons,
I must fight against you from the shadows.'
Thus speaks my master; so much my office.

George II. I have not been angry during this war
until this instant! You tell your master
he must fight us openly in the field
or we will torture captured partisans!
And not a man whom we have yet to seize
shall taste our mercy. Go and tell him so.
>   *[EXIT MESSENGER]*
Why does Babylon's mob support Saddam?
We have given this rabble their freedom,
yet the ingrates fight, rather than thank, us.

Colin. Sire, you can't torture prisoners of war.
It's expressly against the law of arms.
If we are brutal with Saddam's soldiers,
he will be even crueler against ours.

Donald. Our captives aren't legitimate soldiers,

but vile cowards afraid of a fair fight.
They have not earned the rights of prisoners.

Richard. We must be terrible to force our will.
We must both intimidate citizens
and gain key information from them.

George II. Richard and Donald, unleash the furies.
Colin, be prepared to do your duty.
      [EXIT ALL]

[ENTER PRESIDENT, DONALD, AND MAYOR OF FALLUJAH]

George II.   What answer from the Mayor of the town?
This will be his last chance to discuss terms.
Therefore to our best mercy give yourselves
or, like foolish men proud of destruction,
defy us to our worst; for if I must
commence our frontal assault once again,
I will not leave half-conquered Fallujah
until in her ashes she lies buried.
The gates of mercy shall be all shut up,
and the mad soldier, rough and hard of heart,
with bloody hands and conscience wide as hell,
will mow down like grass your fresh, fair virgins
and your innocent, flowering infants.
What is it to me if impious war,
arrayed with red flames like the prince of fiends,
does cruel feats of waste and desolation?
What is it to me if you are the cause
of your maidens falling into the hands
of heated and forcing violation?
What rein can hold licentious wickedness
as it gains force, like a horse bound downhill?
Commanding enraged soldiers to be kind
is as useless as ordering a whale
to come ashore. Thus, men of Fallujah,
take pity on your town and your people
while my soldiers are still in my command;
while the cool and temperate wind of grace
still overblows the filthy, contagious
clouds of murder, pillage, and villainy.
If not – why, in a moment look to see
bloody men, blinded with rage, with foul hands
defile the locks of your shrieking daughters;
take your fathers by their silvery beards,
and dash their reverend heads against walls;

and impale your naked infants on pikes,
while mad mothers break the clouds with their howls.
What say you? Will you yield, and this avoid?
Or, guilty in defense, be thus destroyed?

Mayor.   Dread President, we are Saddam's subjects;
for him, and in his right, we hold this town.
We are determined to survive your siege,
and will not yield our town and lives to you.

      [EXIT MAYOR]

George II.   Come, Donald, you must conquer Fallujah,
then stay here and fortify it for us.
Show no mercy; this town chose not to yield.
The blood it sheds will be on its own hands.

      [EXIT PRESIDENT AND THEN DONALD]

*[ENTER ENVOY, JOHN OF ARIZONA, AND SARAH,
COUNTESS OF ALASKA]*

Envoy. My lords and lady, good health to you all!
I bring you sad tidings from Babylon,
of loss, of slaughter, and discomfiture.
Although our troops easily seized Baghdad,
we declared victory far too early.
Though, after many more months of fighting,
our troops captured Saddam and killed his sons,
his loyalists formed an insurgency,
while oppressed heretics, tasting freedom,
vented hatred on their past oppressors.
We've lost the hearts and minds of the people
through excessive force and needless torture.
Babylon is thus a bloody cauldron.

John. The President has grown unpopular.
Impatient with the war, Americans
have given up on his most noble cause.

Sarah. They fail to see how great their ruler is.
President George, so famous a leader!
We had no President until his time.
We never had a captain of such worth.
Virtue he has; he deserves to command.
His brandished sword does blind men with its beams.
His arms spread wider than a dragon's wings.
His sparkling eyes, replete with wrathful fire,
more dazzle and drive back his enemies
than mid-day sun shining in their faces.
What should I say? His deeds exceed all speech.
He never lifted his hand but conquered.

John. Yet we mourn in black politically.
His name is loathed and never shall revive.
He borrows and spends tons of gold abroad,

while the hungry, angry people at home
hate him so much that I, his party's heir,
lack strength to block Barack's bid for power.

Sarah.   George is a man blessed by the King of Kings,
though to Babylonian insurgents,
the sight of him is more dreadful than Hell.
The battles of the Lord of Hosts he fights.
The faithful's prayers make him prosperous.

John.   Our cause is noble, but is dead for now.
       [EXIT ALL]

Act V. Scene XII.—Washington. The Palace Grounds.

[ENTER BARACK, WHO DROPS TO HIS KNEES]

Barack. Oh Lord, whose captain I account myself,
look on my forces with a gracious eye.
Put in their hands the irons of your wrath,
that they may crush down with a heavy fall
the thick helmets of our adversaries.
Make us your ministers of chastisement,
that we may praise you in the victory.
To you I do commend my watchful soul.
> *[BARACK RISES TO HIS FEET; ENTER COLIN,*
> *SOLDIER, AND ATTENDANTS]*
Fellows in arms, and my most loving friends,
bruised underneath the yoke of tyranny,
thus far into the bowels of the land
have we marched on without impediment;
and here we receive from good old Colin
words of fair comfort and encouragement.

Colin. I was one who helped young George gain the crown;
and yet how I have felt his tyranny.
God guard you hence, young man of Destiny!
Colin, who prophesied that you should reign,
supports your cause, and wants it to flourish.
In God's name, carry on, courageous friends,
to reap a harvest of abiding peace
through this one instance of insurrection.

Barack. Loving countrymen, yet remember this:
God and our good cause fight upon our side.
The prayers of saints stand before our faces.
For who is John of Arizona but
the chosen heir of a bloody tyrant?
Because you fight against God's enemy,
God in justice guards you as his soldiers.
If you do sweat to put a tyrant down,
you sleep in peace, the tyrant being slain.

If you do fight in safeguard of your wives,
your wives shall welcome home the conquerors.
If you do free your children from the sword,
your children's children will thank you someday.
Then, in the name of God and all these rights,
advance your standards, draw your willing swords.
Sound the trumpets boldly and cheerfully;
fight for God and his servant Abraham!

[ENTER SOLDIER]

Soldier. Praise God and your arms, victorious friends:
the day is ours; the bloody dog is done.

Barack. Great God of heaven, say amen to all!
Proclaim a pardon to the soldiers fled
who in submission will return to us.
After taking the holy sacrament,
we will unite the blue states and the red.
America has been a land gone mad,
with regions and families torn apart
by harsh politics led by demagogues.
Oh, now, let our new administration
enrich the time to come with smooth-faced peace,
with smiling plenty and prosperous days!

*[EXIT ALL; ENTER RICHARD OF WYOMING AND
SARAH OF ALASKA]*

Richard. and **Sarah.** *[TOGETHER]*
We shall see about that, foolish young man.

[EXIT RICHARD AND SARAH]